MORE ROCK, COUNTRY AND BACKWARD MASKING UNMASKED

Jacob Aranza

@ 1985

HUNTINGTON HOUSE INC.

Shreveport • Lafayette
Louisiana

Huntington House, Inc.

1200 N. Market Street
Shreveport, Louisiana 71107

Library of Congress Catalog Card Number

85-80776

ISBN Number 0-910311-30-7

Designed by Don Pierce

Printed in the United States of America

To:

Rev. Hardy and Juanita Weathers

This book is dedicated to two people who know very little about rock music, but a lot about the Rock, Christ Jesus. They have walked with him for 50 years and led many down the paths of righteousness. To them I am eternally grateful.

"Music is a curiously subtle art with innumerable, varying emotional connotations. It is made up of many ingredients and, according to the proportions of these components, it can be soothing or invigorating, ennobling or vulgarizing, philosophical or orgiastic.
It has power for evil or for good."

— Dr. Howard Hanson,
American Journal of Psychiatry,
Vol. 99, pg. 317

"ROCK HAS ALWAYS BEEN THE DEVIL'S
MUSIC."

David Bowie
Rolling Stone Magazine
February 12, 1976, pg. 83

"SOME ROCK AND ROLL GROUPS STAND
AROUND IN A CIRCLE AND DRINK CUPS OF
BLOOD. SOME GET ON THEIR KNEES AND
PRAY TO THE DEVIL."

Little Richard
Harrisburg Patriot News, 1980

"AS A COUNTRY ARTIST, I'M NOT PROUD OF
A LOT OF THINGS IN MY FIELD. THERE IS NO
DOUBT IN MY MIND THAT WE ARE
CONTRIBUTING TO THE MORAL DECLINE IN
AMERICA."

Conway Twitty
People Magazine
September 3, 1979, pg. 82

Contents

Chapter 1

More Backward Masking

Backward masking remains as controversial an issue today as it was in 1982 when I wrote my first book *Backward Masking Unmasked* (Huntington House, 1983). Yet while many critics continue to reject the theory that imbedded backward messages are subliminally affecting young people as well as adults, rock groups are continuing to employ the practice.

What critics continue to ignore about the subject of backward masking is that it is a satanic practice taught by the late satanist, Aleister Crowley. In his book *Magick*, which is considered by those in satanism to be one of their sacred books, he instructs those who are learning witchcraft and satanism to learn how to speak, write, and think backwards!

When someone wants to join a satanic coven, they are given a cross which they must turn upside down and break, showing their rejection of the cross. They are also required to say the Lord's Prayer backwards, as a sign of their rejection of Christianity.

The second fact that critics reject, or fail to recognize, is that a majority of the groups that are employing the process of backward masking has been influenced by the teachings of Aleister Crowley, and most by their own admission.

Some critics are quick to say, "This is just a satanic image that groups are using for publicity." May I remind you that Satan will use, and gladly receive, any free advertisement given to him by **anyone**.

In this area I am always reminded of a former satanist high priest who shared with me that he first became intrigued by magic and witchcraft by the seemingly harmless television program "Bewitched." This is the deceptiveness of Satan who has rock stars fooled into saying "It's only an image." Little do they know they are simply like puppets in the hand of Satan. They are like children playing with fire who ignore the fact that fire is hot and will indeed burn you! Whatever the case may be, backward masking is still being used today.

In my first book, *Backward Masking Unmasked*, I shared with you how messages pass the conscious mind and go into the subconscious. If a backward message is imbedded in a song, your conscious mind could not pick it up because it isn't obvious. Yet, at the same time, your subconscious mind could interpret it.

Dr. Wilson Bryan Key, probably the foremost authority on subliminal perception in the Western world, has written three books on the subject.

In his book *Subliminal Seduction* he states, "Experiments have demonstrated that humans can receive, process, and transmit information which makes no conscious appearance at any stage of its passage through their nervous system."

"Indeed," says Key, "the unconscious can operate quite independently from the conscious mechanism in the brain."

Again, in his book *The Clam-Plate Orgy*, when speaking on how to bypass the conscious mind, he states, "The unconscious system appears able to unscramble even kinds of distorted information without individuals becoming consciously aware of the perception."

To give you a very simple example of how a backward message can be perceived, let us examine the eye. Whether you know it, your eye is like a camera. The way you really see things is upside down. Your eye is connected to your brain and one function of the brain is to take what the eye sees and turn it right side up. If this natural process happens every moment you're awake, then why is it so hard to believe that the brain could do the same with what you hear?

Let's examine some of the messages that are found in rock music through backward masking messages that weren't exposed in my first book on the subject.

Motley Crue

This group has writing on their album that openly states THIS ALBUM MAY CONTAIN BACKWARD MESSAGES. They're right too...it does. A segment off their *Shout at the Devil* album, played backwards says, "Backward mask where you are, oh, lost in error, Satan."

Prince

Prince uses backward masking on his ***Purple Rain*** album that mocks the coming of Christ. A segment played backwards says, "Hello, how are you; I'm fine, 'cause I know the Lord is coming soon." Believe me, if Prince knew the Lord was coming soon he wouldn't be doing what he's doing and singing what he's singing!

Quiet Riot

A segment off their ***Metal Health*** album played backwards says, "Serve beast for money."

Rolling Stones

A segment off their ***Tattoo*** album played backwards says "I love you, said the devil."

Led Zeppelin

A segment off their ***House of the Holy*** album played backwards says, "Satan is really lord."

Venom

A segment off their album ***Welcome to Hell*** played backwards says, "It's better to reign in hell than to serve in heaven."

Other groups are using still other subliminal techniques to affect their listeners. The group **Cheap Trick**, on their ***Heaven Tonight*** album, has a place where they say the Lord's Prayer backwards at such a fast speed that is sounds like chipmunks chattering. The group

Blue Oyster Cult also used this same subliminal method on their *Mirrors* album. A segment slowed down to a very low speed becomes "Furthermore, our father who are in heaven Satan."

Earlier in this chapter we made reference to the late satanist Aleister Crowley. Crowley's teachings helped form the basic philosophy that is taught in the Satanic Church of America, headed by Anton LaVey. Crowley was even known to have made human sacrifices in his home. That very home is now owned by Led Zeppelin guitarist, Jimmy Page.

Below are listed some of the rock groups that have openly identified with Aleister Crowley and his teachings in one way or another:

The Beatles
Iron Maiden
Led Zeppelin
Hall and Oates
Ozzy Osbourne
Rolling Stones
Eagles

Many groups no longer feel compelled to hide open references to Satan, sex and drugs. This is true not only of rock and pop but country as well. These are the groups that will be unmasked as you continue to read the following chapters.

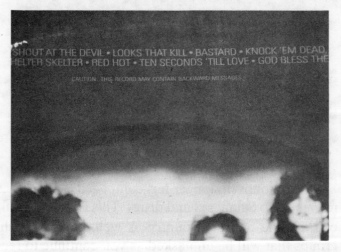

Motley Crue uses backward masking in their *Shout at the Devil* album. The album cover even contains the warning: "Caution: This record may contain backward masking."

Top: Quiet Riot's Metal Health album also has backward messages. *Bottom: Purple Rain* by *Prince* uses backward masking. This album is from *Prince's* feature film debut *Purple Rain* released by Warner Brothers.

The cover of *Led Zeppelin's* album *House of the Holy* depicts naked children on the cover. The album also contains backward messages.

"There's nothing wrong with going around acting like you're God, but you're only going to be God for a year."
— *Eddie Van Halen*

Chapter 2

Music Roots

Some would have you believe that music is just a neutral force. I have had many young people, as well as adults, complain to me and say, "It's only music. It's just another form of art."

Nothing could be further from the truth! The roots of music go far beyond creation or recorded history as we know it. Long before our earth existed, or the first clock of any kind was conceived, there was music. The earliest record we have of music is found in Ezekiel 28:13-17. It reads as follows:

> *Thou hast been in Eden the garden of God; every precious stone was thy covering, the sardius, topaz, and the diamond, the beryl, the onyx, and the jasper, the sapphire, the emerald, and the carbuncle, and gold: the workmanship of thy tabrets and of thy pipes was*

> *prepared in thee in the day that thou wast created. Thou art the anointed cherub (angelic being) that covereth; and I have set thee so; thou wast upon the holy mountain of God; thou hast walked up and down in the midst of the stones of fire. Thou wast perfect in the ways from the day that thou wast created, till iniquity was found in thee. By the multitude of thy merchandise they have filled the midst of thee with violence, and thou hast sinned: therefore I will cast thee as profane out of the mountain of God: and I will destroy thee, O covering cherub, from the midst of the stones of fire. Thine heart was lifted up because of thy beauty, thou hast corrupted thy wisdom by reason of thy brightness: I will cast thee to the ground, I will lay before thee kings, that they may behold thee.*

The Scripture here gives us a short history of Lucifer from his creation to his fall. This passage also makes it clear that when Lucifer was created, a musical ministry was placed in him. A study in the Hebrew reveals that the word for "workmanship" in verse 13 relates to "employment" or "occupation." In the same verse we find references to tabrets, from which we get our drums and tambourines, as well as reference to pipes, such as flutes or woodwind instruments.

Lucifer is the only angelic being mentioned in the Bible to possess a musical ministry. At one point in time, he used his musical abilities for God's purposes, but now he uses them to exalt evil and draw men away from God. Having been created with musical abilities, it is not hard to believe that Satan indeed influences music today!

It is clear that music has direct relation to the spirit, and was created by God for his purposes. It is a spiritual force and Satan knows what a powerful tool it is in the lives of people. It can make you laugh, or it can make you cry. It can arouse you sexually, or it can make you feel empty and depressed. It can excite you enough to make you want to exercise, or can discourage you enough to make you want to drink. Yes, music is genuinely a powerful force and that's why Satan has used it so much. He once had a music ministry for the almighty God; the only angelic musician God chose to mention in the Bible. Unfortunately, he still has a music ministry, but it is used to tear down, destroy and mislead humanity.

Only two purposes for music's creation can be found in the Bible. The one purpose is to glorify God and further his kingdon, the other is to glorify evil and further Satan's kingdom.

As for glorifying God, we find a multitude of Scriptures concerning singing songs of thanksgiving, praise and remembrances unto the Lord. We even read that what we sing has a spiritual effect on those who hear.

In 1 Samuel 16:23 we read about King Saul who was troubled by an evil spirit. David, who was known for his spiritual songs to the Lord, would play those songs on the harp for King Saul. This was the only time that the evil spirit would leave the king and he would have rest for his soul!

When it comes to glorifying evil through music and furthering Satan's kingdom, we find many instances where rebellious, worldly people would be playing music.

Party music goes back a long way! Ever since Lucifer's fall, music that incites the flesh to fulfill its lusts, and encourages mankind to sin has always been played. In the same way, this music has a spiritual effect on the hearers.

In Exodus 32:6 and 18 we find Moses coming down from the mountain after receiving the Ten Commandments from the Lord to find the people at a large rock concert. They were dancing naked while singing and worshipping a golden calf. This music promoted evil and turned these God-fearing people into savage sinners. Satan, then, as today, was the unseen spiritual force behind it all.

Almighty God is the original creator of music, and music that is inspired, ordained and approved of him will have positive effects in the lives of those who listen to it. Satan was originally created with a music ministry in the kingdom of God, and now uses his talents to negatively affect the lives of those who will listen cautiously. So be aware of the spirit of the music you listen to.

> *"Crucifixes are very sexy because there's a naked man on them."*
> — *Madonna*

Chapter 3

Satan's Agenda

Agenda: A schedule or outline to be brought before a council.

Many may find it hard to believe that Satan has an agenda, not only for people's lives, but also for their music. For many, it's even difficult to believe there's really a devil, Lucifer, or Satan. Yes, Satan, who once led the greatest rebellion the heavenlies has ever seen, taking with him one-third of the angels, has once again outlined his plan to deceive and destroy. He continues to seek to exalt himself as supreme in the universe, any way he can.

Recently, one of America's most popular youth evangelists was on a plane flying to a crusade. Everything seemed as though it would be a typical flight. Little did he know today he would peek into Satan's agenda for the music world. As the plane became airborne, he began to talk with the man seated beside him.

After the normal small talk, the evangelist asked the gentleman in what business he was involved. To his surprise, the man was the manager of one of the largest rock groups in the world. The evangelist then asked, "What's next in the rock music world?"

As the manager of the rock group began to talk, the evangelist was shocked by his knowledge, not only about rock music, but also about the sales and marketing industry. The man proceeded to tell him about the **Four Step Plan** taking place in rock music. This is what I call "Satan's Agenda" for the music world.

He explained that each phase or step in this agenda appealed to a different side of the human personality. He said that Step One began in 1955, at the birth of rock music and lasted until 1965. This step was intended to push sex through music. Elvis Presley, Chuck Berry and Gene Vincent helped to accomplish this through their sex appeal. This promotion of sex, from 1955-1965, brought on the sexual revolution and the free love generation. Young people across America, and around the world, threw away their moral standards so they could both listen to this music and experience it. This was to open the door for Step Two which began in 1965.

Step Two was to run from 1965-1970. He said that this phase was meant to arouse the spirit of young people towards drugs, rebellion and anti-establishment movements. Protests began to develop on campuses across the nation. A rejection of all traditional values evolved, and an arousal of the spirit world through the supernatural began.

Many remember groups like **The Beatles** turning to gurus and Eastern religions. This spiritual awakening through music gave way to millions turning to cults, like the Children of God, Hare Krishna, Ma Jura Ja Gi and many others.

Step Three, he continued, began in 1970 and has run through part of the '80s. In this step, the quality of music isn't important, but that it has an addicting sound with loud and violent tones.

He went on to say, "We're just like any other business. How does a business sell cosmetics, clothes or cars? They all have what is called a motivational trigger. You touch someone's hot button and they buy. In rock music we have been looking for the ultimate hot button for years and we believe we have finally found it!" He explained this to be part of Step Four.

Step Four will begin during the '80s. "We have found," he said, "that the greatest commitment anyone makes is a religious one. That would be the greatest motivator to get people to buy rock records. So, beginning in the '80s, we are going to have religious services in our concerts. We are going to pronounce ourselves (rock stars) as messiahs, making intimate acquaintances and covenants with Satan. We'll be praying for the sick, raising people up out of wheelchairs and performing the supernatural during concerts. We are going to be worshipped!"

Is it any wonder, then, that the rock group **Black Sabbath** has been known to make altar calls to Lucifer in some of their concerts? Stevie Nicks, of **Fleetwood Mac**, is known for dedicating their concerts to the witches of the world.

A youth pastor who went to an **Iron Maiden** concert in Portland, Oregon, shared with me that their first words were "Welcome to Satan's Sanctuary."

On their album *Welcome to Hell,* the new rock group **Venom** has the following words printed in bold

letters on the back of their album. "WE ARE POS-
SESSED BY ALL THAT'S EVIL. THE DEATH
OF YOUR GOD WE DEMAND: WE SPIT AT
THE VIRGIN YOU WORSHIP, AND SIT AT
THE LORD SATAN'S LEFT HAND."

Satan's agenda is being unfolded before our very
eyes. All of this may come as somewhat of a shock
to you, but it's no surprise to the rock stars of today.
The famous rock star **Ozzy Osbourne** is quoted as
saying, "Rock is a religion."

While recently speaking in Sweden, I happened to
be there at the same time that **David Bowie** was giving
a concert. One evening on Swedish television they
began interviewing people who were sleeping in tents
for days, literally relieving themselves openly on the
streets in freezing weather, just to get a ticket to hear
David Bowie. The reporter, puzzled at the radical
commitment just to hear David Bowie, asked one of
the teenagers why he would go through all of this for
just one concert. His response was, "Because David
Bowie is God"!

[1] *Power Behind Music,* Terry Law

Top: Venom's album *Welcome to Hell* includes this picture with strong occult overtones. *Bottom: Healing* by Todd Rundgren includes one song entitled "Tiny Demons."

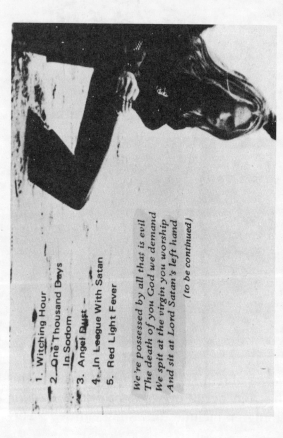

1. Witching Hour
2. One Thousand Days In Sodom
3. Angel Dust
4. In League With Satan
5. Red Light Fever

We're possessed by all that is evil
The death of you God we demand
We spit at the virgin you worship
And sit at Lord Satan's left hand
(to be continued)

Venom, a new rock group, has printed in bold letters on the back of their *Welcome to Hell* album: **"WE ARE POSSESSED BY ALL THAT'S EVIL. THE DEATH OF YOUR GOD WE DEMAND: WE SPIT AT THE VIRGIN YOU WORSHIP, AND SIT AT LORD SATAN'S LEFT HAND."**

*"Organized religion is something
I'm very disappointed in.
I consider myself religion."*
— *Kenny Rogers*

Chapter 4

Country Music:
Behind Closed Doors

What once was commonly considered to be a private matter discussed only behind closed doors, has been the major theme of country music for sometime.

Rock, though filled with satanism, sex and drug references, still has a hard time keeping up with the cheatin', drinkin', and one night stands that continue to dominate country music. I am always amazed by the God-fearing parents who become outraged when they hear me speak about rock music and its evils, while their consciences remain unbothered about their listening to country music, which is often far worse than rock has ever been.

The majority of country music's lyrics can be traced to these three major areas: sex, divorce and drinking. I happen to believe that country music is more damaging than rock because society approves of sex, divorce and drinking, but rock often talks of things which aren't so easily accepted, such as satanism and drugs.

Dr. James Schaefer, Ph.D., Director of the University of Minnesota's office of alcohol and other drug abuse programming, has discovered that country music can lead to alcoholism among listeners. He stated in an US Magazine interview, "I used to think the faster the beat, the faster the sipping. But after a little research, I discovered something that bartenders have known all along: the slower the beat, the faster the sip."

Using graduate student volunteers, Schaefer (who also teaches anthropology at the University) haunted bars in Montana and Minnesota. Scientifically taping the number of sips per minute, with the number of beats per song, the following results were computed:

"It took me only three consecutive Friday nights to find out that there's definitely a correlation between high-risk country and western songs and drinking, especially those of Kenny Rogers, Waylon Jennings and Hank Williams. So if you listen too many times to Kenny Rogers' 'Lucille', or other high-risk songs, you can end up plastered."

Schaefer defines high-risk songs as having 50 to 60 beats per minute.

Other examples include Crystal Gayle's "Don't It Make My Brown Eyes Blue," Johnny Paycheck's "Take This Job And Shove It" and almost any Hank Williams song.

Many country artists like George Jones are known for their much publicized drinking. Jones has been known to not even show up for some of his concerts, due to heavy drinking.

A phrase from a new Gatlin Brothers song says, "If there's no Mogen David (a brand of wine) in heaven, then who the hell wants to go." Larry Gatlin recently turned himself into a drug abuse center for rehabilitation.

As though this wouldn't be enough, many country stars even boast of drug abuse.

A recent press release about Johnny Paycheck's upcoming album had this to say: "He doesn't apologize for his bad-boy 'out-law' image or drug use. 'Yes, I do cocaine, but cocaine isn't a killer drug and neither is alcohol. Heroin is a problem. P.C.P. is a killer drug. Cocaine and alcohol are OK upfront drugs.' "

In a copyright story in *The Tennessean*, Paycheck said that his career troubles, including a string of criminal charges, debts and missed shows, should be blamed on the country music industry.

In December 1981, Paycheck was arrested on a charge of molesting a 12-year-old girl after a concert in Wyoming. He denied the charge which was later dropped.

Even the famed Merle Haggard confesses to smoking grass (marijuana) and heavy partying.[2]

Any questions as to whether this music has an affect on people's lives can be answered by merely looking to the lives of the artists themselves. Many have swapped husbands and wives about as often as they swap record labels.

Conway Twitty stated in a *People Magazine* interview[3], "As a country artist, I'm not proud of a lot of things in my field. There is no doubt in my mind that we are contributing to the moral decline in America."

What seems to be a greater disgrace than all of this, is the fact that many of the artists now performing country music and living what they sing, were once gospel music singers. They started out sincerely wanting to please God with their talent but eventually sold out their commitment to Christ for money.

Here are the names of some groups who started out in gospel music:

The Gatlin Brothers
The Statler Brothers
The Oak Ridge Boys
Janie Fricke
The Thrashers
Ricky Scaggs
Willie Nelson
Dolly Parton
Elvis Presley
Randy Owens (Alabama)
The Bellamy Brothers

The real story of country music can also be told by the titles of the songs themselves:

"Loving Up a Storm"
"You'd Make An Angel Want to Cheat"
"That Lovin' You Feelin' Again"
"You Make Me Want to be a Mother"
"Behind Closed Doors"
"Something to Brag About"
"She's Pullin' Me Back Again"
"Making Love From Memory"
"Let's Get It While the Gettin's Good"
"She's Not Really Cheatin,' She's Just Gettin' Even"
"Heavenly Bodies"
"Makin' Love Don't Always Make Love Grow"
"First Time Around"
"When I Get My Hands on You"
"I Feel Like Lovin' You Again"
"Why Don't You Spend the Night?"

"War is Hell on the Home Front Too"
"I May be Used, But Baby I Ain't Used Up"
"To All The Girls I've Loved Before"
"When We Make Love"
"Let's Stop Talkin' About It" •
"I Dream of Women Like You"
"Just Give Me One More Night" •
"Now I Lay Me Down To Cheat" •

The Raleigh, North Carolina, News and Observer said it best when they stated, "Honky tonk angels and cheatin' men have always played their part in country songs, but never in the history of country music have their illicit affairs been so graphically depicted as they are today."

I would add that all secular music is getting worse in lyrical content. With just the limited amount of information that I have given you in this chapter, it is very plain to see that country music is a powerful tool in the hands of Satan. No Christian should be filling his or her hearts and minds with country music's themes.

At a time when there is so much sin and immorality in our country, we don't need any more input concerning sex, divorce and drinking. The worst part of it all is that country music's stronghold is mainly with adults.

If parents are to be the example that God requires them to be and they fail in this area, then Satan has not only destroyed the convictions of the parents, but of the children as well.

Remember what the Bible says in Galatians 6:7, "Don't be deceived; God is not mocked. Whatever a man sows, that shall he also reap."

If you, as a parent, don't want your children

listening to immoral rock music, then don't listen to immoral country music. If you don't want your children going to sex-filled movies, then don't go to them yourself.

Let me also mention that movies don't have to be R-rated to be sex-filled. What used to be R-rated is now PG-rated, and what used to be X-rated is now R-rated. God only knows what the X-rated movies are like! If you don't want your children interested in immorality, then don't whet their appetites by watching adulterous and sinful relationships on TV soaps and sit-coms.

All that most modern music is doing is giving words and melody to what most people are filling their minds with through television. Many may beg to differ with me on these views concerning country music. If you do, I would encourage you to examine the Top-100 country songs in America today. As you read the titles, be honest with yourself about what's really being promoted in the music, and ask yourself if these themes help make the quality of your life better.

[1] *US Magazine,* March 31, 1981

[2] *US Magazine,* November 21, 1983, pg. 53

[3] *People Magazine,* September 3, 1979, pg. 82

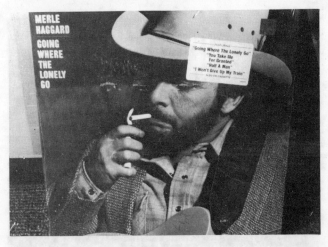

Top: Merle Haggard says he is heavy into partying and smokes marijuana. *Bottom: Jerry Lee Lewis'* singing career has been plagued and nearly destroyed by his lifestyle.

Top: Honky Tonkin' is a favorite theme of country music lyrics. *Bottom: The Oak Ridge Boys*, popular recording artists, started their careers in gospel music.

Top: Recording artist ***George Jones,*** well known for his drinking, recorded one album entitled ***Bartender's Blues.*** ***Bottom: Larry Gatlin and the Gatlin Brothers Band*** has one release with the following lyrics: "If there's no Mogen David (wine) in heaven then who the hell wants to go." Larry Gatlin recently sought help for drug abuse.

> *"Video music is a well-rounded*
> *satanic education, and I can say*
> *that with no reservations."*
> — John Gradick

Chapter 5

MTV

Throw down your earphones and wipe off your eyeglasses! That music you have been praying would be taken off radio has now invaded television!

Rock music, after going through its largest slump in its 30 year history, has finally found a savior. After almost losing the battle with Pac Man, Donkey Kong and other video games, rock has played its ultimate ace. The battle was not only for attention, but for the favorite god of this world: the Almighty Dollar.

After being knocked down and given the mandatory "eight count", rock has counter attacked with a blow so strong it would even make the famed "Rocky Balboa" shiver. The blow I am speaking of is the marriage of video and the quadraphonic stereo.

This combination has produced an uncontrollable medium that attacks the two greatest human senses: sight and sound. Why is this so important? Simply because your mind remembers 95 percent of what you receive by sight and sound, as compared to remembering only 3-5 percent of what you receive solely by hearing. This union has brought rock profits from the lowest valley to the highest mountain.

An example was given by Michele Peacock, who oversees E.M.I's video promotional department:[1] "I'd been working in the field in the South and Southwest, where they did have MTV in markets like Dallas and Tulsa. And almost instantly, after MTV came on there, something funny began to happen. **Duran Duran's** album, with no radio play, (and with a band who were already popular in England and Europe, and who'd been touring and touring here to no apparent gain) was selling like hotcakes wherever they had MTV. We checked into it and, sure enough, the band had a video or two on MTV; and our accounts at retail (referring to record stores) were calling us with wild stories about kids who'd come into the stores saying, 'I saw this band on MTV. . .' and they were buying the record."

Another example to illustrate the power of MTV is the group **Cheap Trick**.[2] This is an established American band with a solid following. In 1982 they released an album, *One on One*, that did its usual strong initial sales to its regular audience, though not exceeding their average sales quota. Radio simply wasn't giving their songs a lot of air play. The album began to die on the vine, dropping right off the charts.

Then videos were made of two songs off the album, "If You Want My Love," and "She's Tight." MTV put them into top rotation. As a result, the radio play and sales shot right back up.

"This really opened our eyes," said Susan Blond of Epic Records.

With these types of results, you can see why record

companies are spending up to hundreds of thousands of dollars on one single video. One would think that demonstrating songs on video would have some limitations, but MTV has proven that all the sexual, violent and satanic themes of rock can be graphically portrayed over the tube. Some videos even contain total nudity.

In the video by the **Pointer Sisters**, "I'm So Excited," there is one segment of nudity from the waist down. Another song, "Girls on Film," contains close-up full frontal nudity. David Bowie's "China Girl" video shows him having sex with a naked girl on the beach. Van Halen's "Pretty Woman" video was removed from MTV because the station received scores of complaints about the transvestism and the exploitation of women. Of course all of this is nothing new to the rock industry. It's always pushed the public's conscience to the limit.

Now let's get an inside view of video music from John Gradick. John was a host for the Atlanta Video Music Channel, which broadcasts into 4.2-million homes. He interviewed some 200 rock stars. His list includes **Duran Duran, Boy George** and **The Culture Club, W.A.S.P., Adam and the Ants,** and many others. After several years as a disc jockey (DJ) and two years as a video disc jockey (VDJ), he has some genuine insights into the effect of music on people's lives and he encouraged me to share them with you.

A message from John Gradick:

"Rock video is the last dying attempt for record labels to make money, because record sales have become so bad. The 'heavy metal' tapes that receive airplay are nothing but women in bondage chains and are used to arouse you sexually. There are no laws on video music or cable. You can show anything you want because it's not broadcast over the airwaves. I stopped my own children from watching rock videos when I wasn't even a Christian! Even if I was the one that was hosting the program, they would always fight and couldn't play together. If they were affected so much as two- and three-year-olds, what do you think it does to teenagers?

"I wish you could see the change I've seen in young people under the influence of music videos. So many teenagers are so deceived. They won't let go of their rock and roll for anything. If they could only see that rock stars don't care about them even if they are their fans. They don't care if you graduate from high school, or if you have a good family. They could care less! They'll never meet you. The only reason they love their fans is because their fans buy their records. The record industry has nothing more on their mind than earning money. They talk about art forms, but all they care about is money.

"Many of the rock groups don't even know what they're dabbling in. They get on the show business train and find out the person they're sitting next to is Satan!

"The group **Grim Reaper** has a video called 'See You in Hell My Friend'. Ronnie James Dio said in an interview that he had an experience with the 'dark side' and it showed him he didn't want to mess with it. Yet, at the same time, he has a picture on his album of a god-like statue of Satan in the fiery pit leading to hell.

"Look at Boy George. He is a homosexual drag queen that America has embraced, who couldn't even make it in England. He had to come to America to get accepted and make money.

"Video music is the biggest poison around because you don't have to go to a rock concert to be exposed to it. It comes right into your house. The thing that bothers me about video music is that Satan doesn't have to hide himself anymore. The children are accepting him and the parents are just turning their heads."

After reading this message from John, you can see there has been a change in his life. Just a few months ago, John committed his life to Jesus Christ. One week later he was given my tape on rock music by the owner of a Chistian bookstore where the tape is sold. John told me he left the tape lying in his house for about two weeks. One evening, John and his wife listened to the tape just before going to sleep. As the tape continued to play, John became very convicted by the Holy Spirit and he and his wife jumped out of bed and destroyed their entire album collection. He also quit being a VDJ for the Atlanta Rock Video Channel.

[1] *The Rolling Stone Book of Rock Video,* pg. 88-91

[2] Ibid #1

"Music has the power to form character."
— Aristotle

Chapter 6

Guidelines For Christian Music

Today there are as many controversial views on styles of Christian music as there are non-Christian music.

One of the questions I'm most frequently asked is about Christian music styles. There are those who feel like anyone who is singing with a sincere heart, no matter what the music sounds like (be it country, rock, or punk) are all right if they're doing it unto the Lord.

Then there are those who feel that any music dealing with electric guitars, drums or blaring synthesizers is not acceptable, and perhaps even sinful. Many who hold this view seem only to be comfortable with southern gospel and country-flavored solos.

By and large, the Christian community has adopted country music, baptized it, and come up with southern gospel music. Yet many of these same advocates become outraged when young people do the same with their favorite flavor of music.

I don't agree with either of these. I believe that instead of looking for a certain style, we should first look for content. There are some Christian artists who have dared to be different and sing a new song unto the Lord, which doesn't sound like a warmed-over Top Ten hit with new words. With them I rejoice as they continue to look to the Chief Musician for inspiration.

One great disappointment in the Christian music industry is that many artists go out into the world to find styles and gimmicks that will appeal to their audiences. There are artists who actually go to worldly concerts, or watch popular television programs, to get ideas for their music. What a reproach this is to our Lord, who has made his creativity and divine inspiration available to us. May God help us to tap into his creativity so that our music won't just be an echo of the world.

In this context, I would like to give a few guidelines for the music that you do listen to. Take a moment and look at it this way: would you listen to this music if you were in the Throne Room in heaven with the Almighty God?

You may say, "But I'm not in heaven' I'm here on earth." That's true, but, nevertheless, the Bible tells us, "In Him we live, and move, and have our being" (Acts 17:28). We exist in the very presence of God, and should be living as though we are serving him in his presence.

After a time of prayer one morning, I wanted to listen to some music that would assist me in my praise and worship to the Lord. I put on one of my albums, which are all Christian artists, and only had it on a minute before I realized that it wasn't helping me worship the Lord. So I put on another and another album in search of one that would help me worship the Lord.

This taught me many things. For one thing, I learned that all Christian music is not worship music. Some of it is to convict us of sin, or to exhort us to live holy lives, or to comfort us. We need to understand the difference and listen to the music that will meet our need at the time we listen to it.

Another thing I found was that there is some music I was listening to just because I liked the style and the beat. In this respect we have to be careful that there is a clear, divinely inspired purpose behind the music, and that we don't just buy Christian albums because the style appeals to us.

There are three tests I use in deciding what music I am going to listen to:

The Motive

What is the motivation, or reason, why the artist (or artists) is in the music industry?

One friend of mine, in the gospel-music field, told me that many artists are involved in Christian music simply because they couldn't make it in secular music. It is commonly known by Christian music promoters that some artists are involved in drinking and immorality, just like musicians of the world. This isn't true of the majority of them, but the fact that it is true of ANY of them should make us concerned with the motivation behind the artist.

Some artists feel that just because they are singing Christian themes, their music is approved of God.

The problem is that anyone can vocalize Christian themes (remember the Doobie Brothers' "Jesus Is

Just All Right With Me"), but this does not mean it is approved of God. God's seal of approval is the annointing of his Spirit. When musicians are acting in obedience to God, their music will change your life. It will encourage you in your Christian walk and will expand your experience with the Lord, making you draw closer to him and farther away from carnality and the lusts of the world. When this results from the music we listen to, we can be sure that this person is acting with a pure motive towards God.

The Method

The method is simply what style or type of music the person is using. Here is where most controversy lies. Some people feel you should only use certain instruments, while others feel that any instrument played unto the Lord is fine. My personal conviction is that any method can be used to exalt Christ, but the method should never distract or take away from the message. The method should enhance, adorn or accent the message.

When the focus is drawn away from the message to the music, the musician becomes another music star and becomes the main attraction in place of the Lord. In such cases, Jesus just becomes the platform for the musician to display the flesh. This would be like Jesus riding into Jerusalem on a donkey and the people applauding the donkey. How foolish and sad.

The Message

This is the most important of the three. For music to be truly Christian, there must be a clear message in each song, which should encourage you to godly living.

Many gospel artists attempt to have "crossover" songs, meaning that they are songs that could be played over both Christian and secular radio stations. These crossover songs avoid directly speaking about Christ, and use lyrics that "shadow" Christianity. The tragedy with this is that it is a form of man's wisdom, for even some secular songs could be made to sound like they're "kinda Christian."

If we make our message so similar sounding to theirs, then we're telling them they can get saved and stay the way they are. This is diluting the gospel which is supposed to be proclaimed in the power of God's Spirit. Proclaiming a diluted gospel will produce diluted Christians.

I am reminded of the story in the Old Testament about the messenger who could run very fast. One day, a slower messenger was given a message to take to a king. The faster messenger then outran him to get to the king first. Upon arriving at the palace, the messenger was asked "What is the message?" to which he replied, "I don't have it, but I got here first!"

May we never run the race without a message. In this sense it is important to recognize that in the music we listen to there must be a clear, sound message.

Chapter 7

Questions Most Asked

In my daily mail there are many typical questions that seem to be on the minds and hearts of numerous young readers, as well as adults. This chapter is designed to answer many of these questions that you may be asking.

QUESTION: I know what you say about the groups in your book is true, but you didn't mention my favorite group. What about them?
ANSWER: I may not have spoken about your favorite rock or country group, but if their goal isn't to glorify God and help build his kingdom, then their music will hinder and distract you from serving God, and can easily provoke you to rebel against God.

QUESTION: The groups I like don't sing about

Satan, sex, or drugs. What's wrong with listening to them?

ANSWER: Just because a group doesn't openly sing about immorality doesn't mean their music is approved by God. If the music you're listening to doesn't come from the heart of a spiritual Christian artist, you are opening the door to carnality, humanism and demonic forces. It will distract you from serving him, feed self-centeredness, and eventually breed rebellion in your heart. Just because something appears to be good doesn't mean it is good. (2 Cor. 11:14)

QUESTION: I don't really like what a lot of rock groups sing about, but I don't listen to the words. I just like the music. Isn't that OK?

ANSWER: It might be OK if you didn't have a spirit or a brain. You may not realize it, but you are more than a physical body. You also have a mind and a spirit which both respond to music. Your mind is like a computer and absorbs what it hears, including words to music. It can't be avoided since your brain takes and stores the information you hear and receive through your senses. Your spirit also responds to music because God created music as a spiritual force. If you are a Christian, the Spirit of Christ dwells in your spirit, making you sensitive to God's voice and will. When you listen to music that isn't inspired by God, it dulls your sensitivity to God. Eventually it will breed rebellion in you. It's a lot like smoking cigarettes. They will make you an addict and give you cancer, killing the life in you. This is Satan's ultimate plan for music, no matter how innocent it may sound.

QUESTION: Isn't there music that is just neutral, not good or bad?

ANSWER: No. Consider this: there is no such thing as a man who is neutral concerning God. Jesus said people are either against him or for him. Man was created with the purpose to glorify his Creator and have fellowship with him. Even so, music is the same way. Its ultimate purpose from creation has been to glorify God and all that he is. Music either encourages godliness, or discourages godliness; there is no neutral ground.

QUESTION: What about instrumental music?

ANSWER: Concerning this subject I would like to quote someone known to have specialized in instrumental music. While I was speaking in Louisville, Kentucky, the pastor shared with me that Phil Driscoll had been there the previous week. Phil Driscoll was in secular music for many years as a writer and instrumentalist, making up to $450,000 a year previous to his conversion to Christ. Phil shared that he felt the spirit of whoever was playing the music was the spirit that would influence those who listened to it. I agree with this.

I might add that there are plenty of instrumental albums produced by Christian artists, from jazz to classical, and from pop to easy listening. There's really no excuse for listening to secular music anymore. Whether the music has words, the spiritual force behind it will affect you.

QUESTION: How can we judge rock stars? Doesn't the Bible say that we shouldn't judge others?

ANSWER: This may seem like a silly question, but it is one that I am frequently asked. Yes, the Bible says that we shouldn't judge others, but the "others" it is referring to are Christians; not the unsaved. Paul confronted the church in 1 Corinthians 6:3 saying that they should at least be able to judge among themselves knowing that we will one day judge the angels. As Christians we're responsible to examine the result (or fruit) of a thing, to see what the root really is. We're expected to judge something to see if it is of God.

QUESTION: I know my music is not pleasing to God and I really want to give it up, but it's hard. How do I do it?

ANSWER: If you're a Christian, and honestly have a repentant heart regarding the music you listen to, you must act on your conviction. In both Matthew 3:8 and Acts 26:20 we are told to act, or do deeds, that show our repentance. In this situation, you should gather all your records and cassettes together. Then ask God to give you the power and the grace to destroy them. Ask God to show you how much this music has misled you and hurt him. Then ask him to forgive you and wash your mind and spirit afresh in the blood of Jesus Christ. Last of all, begin to vocally thank him for what he has forgiven you of and for the new desires he is going to place in your heart concerning music.

QUESTION: What kind of music should I listen to?

ANSWER: You should listen to music that glorifies God, his character, and that encourages you to godly living. Listen to music that has clear spiritual content. Listen to music that makes you aware of God's presence in your life.

QUESTION: Well, who gave you the right to tell me what kind of music is right or wrong?

ANSWER: No one has given me the right to tell you what is right or wrong. All I can do is give you guidelines from God's Word, the Bible. You personally need to allow God to speak to your own heart about what music you're listening to. Pray and ask God about your music. He still answers prayer.

QUESTION: I don't like non-Christian music, but I work in a place where it is played all day long. What should I do?

ANSWER: You can start by expressing your views to your boss. Let him know that the major themes of the music are sex, drinking, drugs and satanism. Try to get them to play instrumental music, and offer to bring in your own instrumental music. They'd probably like the Christian instrumental music and wouldn't be offended since there aren't any words. If you can't get rid of the secular music, then be sure to keep a song in your heart that you sing to the Lord. Ask God each day to protect you from the negative forces behind this music. No matter what happens, have confidence that God will give you the power to be victorious in this situation.

Chapter 8

The Mailbox

Dear Mr. Aranza,

Your book *Backward Masking Unmasked* woke me up to the fact that I have been a part of "rock-n-roll religion" for most of my teen years. I was a member of a rock and roll group and although I didn't do drugs or drink, I was greatly influenced from the moral standpoint. I now realize that rock groups don't intentionally worship Satan, but are serving him just by being into rock. I know it's going to be tough to give it up, but I know that I need to serve the Lord and do whatever is necessary to do so.

Sincerely,

W.F., Iowa

Dear Mr. Aranza,

My mother picked up your book **Backward Masking Unmasked** for my sisters and I. I am familiar with many of the rock groups and songs. I am also very moved with your book and have decided to stop listening to rock music.

Sincerely Yours,

J.G., Maryland

Dear Jacob,

I just finished reading your book **Backward Masking Unmasked.** I must admit that I was shocked at all the groups involved in this and I am sure that there are many more. I have been born again for about one and one-half years, but I was still listening to rock music. Well, not any more! I have about 400 albums that are going in the trash and they will be broken and smashed so that no one wil be able to listen to them. My radio is now on AM WEZE and WROL; the only stations in the area that have Christian programs. The thought of listening to rock turns me completely off now!

In Christ,

K.B., MA

Dear Mr. Aranza,

I read your book about backward masking and I want to thank you for writing it. After reading your book, and another like it, I dedicated my life to the Lord.

Love,

⤺ K.R., North Carolina

Dear Jacob,

Praise God for your book *Backward Masking Unmasked*. It helped me get born again! I had gone to church for 12 years and had become very "religious." I loved rock and roll music. It became my attention at school, my comfort at night, my pride and sex. I started enjoying this music, and I wanted to dance so I did. Oh, it only started when I was in the privacy of my bedroom. A few years later, it took me to booze, bars, and the "gay lifestyle." I centered my life around strip shows and getting attention.

I had your book for over six months. I decided to read it one day. Then it dawned on me that Satan had entrapped me just by listening to music.

God Bless You!

T.L., Arkansas

Dear Mr. Aranza,

After going to the Christian bookstore, my sister (who was with me) showed me a book she purchased. It had to do with unmasking rock and roll music. That evening she began to read the book and by the time it was time to go to bed she had finished it. The book opened her eyes to what some groups do with their music. As I end this letter, the most exciting part was the next evening she destroyed every record album she had! I truly feel that breaking the records was the first step for her. He has so much more for her now that she has chosen to follow him.

In God's love,

L.B., Connecticut

Dear Mr. Aranza,

I read your book *Backward Masking Unmasked* today at school. It did shock me, frighten me, and enlighten me, but it did not change me. I got home from school and went right back to "my music." I am a 15-year-old sophomore, not your typical "rocker," I make A's and B's at school, I have <u>never</u> done drugs, or been involved with anyone sexually. All of my friends are dedicated Christians, and I attend church every Sunday and regular church activities with them, but I always can't wait to get home and get back to "my music" (rock and roll). My friends don't approve of it; they suggest I read your book. So how did I get so wrapped up in rock and roll, you say. Well, I grew up with it. I know practically everything about today's artists and bands (musically) and I buy *Circus* magazine on a regular basis (monthly). My brothers both have a drum set and an electric guitar and their dream is to "be like them (other bands) someday." I have been to a couple of rock concerts with them and, for the most part, I enjoyed them. When I read your book, and it came out about the satanic church and witchcraft, etc., . . . I was shocked, but I still have every desire and urge I have ever had to listen to rock and roll. It's a <u>part</u> of me, a very <u>big</u> part of me. My friends don't understand it, I just tell them, "I guess that's one thing that will always separate us, the music." God is a very big part of my life, but I guess music is bigger, it's my dream! I have thought about being like Cyndi Lauper or Madonna, and maybe someday I will be. I listen to hard rock, too. (*Ozzy Osbourne, Motley Crue, W.A.S.P., Twisted Sister, Ratt, Van Halen,* etc. . .) It's normal; every teenager loves rock and roll, even when my parents were growing up they listened to rock and roll. It's been around for years! In your book you said you had to change. How did you do it? That's a lot of will power, I mean I just can't see myself giving up one of the biggest and most important things in my life right now. I don't even know if I want to quit listening to it (pretty wrapped up, huh?). But I do believe what you said. It's just that I've always heard "never give up your dreams." What's wrong with that? I am interested if you can help me out, and your response would be greatly appreciated.

Sincerely,

S.R.

Dear Jacob,

Thank you so much for helping me and thousands of other young people. My aunt got me your book and I have read it twice. I now have rock and roll out of my system!

Sincerely yours,

M.T.

Dear Mr. Aranza,

For years I've had preachers preach about the bad

effects of "rock music." I was always told that I shouldn't listen to it, but did I listen to what I was told? NO WAY! I hate being told what to do! I knew rock music was drawing me away from the Lord, but I couldn't bring myself to do anything about it. Finally, my youth leader gave me your book. I said, "Oh no, I might get convicted," and sure enough I did! I just thank the Lord that I was open-minded when I read your book, because I am usually <u>very</u> hardheaded! I quit listening to rock music last week. Since then, I have received what I've been longing for, for a long time: a closer walk with God!

Thank you,

J.B.

Dear Jacob,

I have felt compelled to write to you for about two weeks now; ever since my two boys and I read your book *Backward Masking Unmasked*. What an eye-opener! I am grateful for your knowledge and inspiration to write this informative book. Both my boys were very interested in the book and have shared it with several friends. (They are 18 and 14 years old). They both felt led to destroy numerous albums, cassettes, and 45s. PRAISE GOD!

God Bless You!

P.C., Kentucky

Dear Mr. Aranza,

It seemed for many years that no one really cared about what happened to me, so I took to rock when

I was really young. I read in all of the rock magazines that the rock groups really cared about their fans, and that made me feel good and wanted, like I really mattered. I now see all they cared about was the money, not me. It's great to know that someone like you thinks I matter. Thank you and God bless you,

T.F., Michigan

Mr. Aranza,

Don't bother prayin' for me 'cause it's a waste of time. Don't waste your breath. He's dead, man, even I know he died on the cross. Dead, and you shouldn't talk to a dead man. Oh, by the way, I got a picture of the real god. The God you pray to is dead. The heavy metal god isn't. In the picture you see the guy with the arrow pointing to him? The guy with the cross? He could be a god, I think he is! Rock itself is like a god. It's all powerful, man. Acid rock, rock rock, every minute of the day! I live for rock and I luv it!

Bye,

G.

Dear Jacob,

I accepted Jesus Christ as my Savior in early 1980. In my devotions I've asked God to give me some real "proof" that *KISS* is what you're trying to make them out to be, but so far no "proof." So I've stuck with the group ever since the fifth grade, and am currently the president of a local chapter of the official *KISS* fan club, the KISS ARMY.

As far as their music goes, like they said before, they don't preach anything. So their songs are not trying to get any kind of message across, the music is just music. This next quote I have taken from an interview on the cable TV network USA. "Rock and roll is made up basically of two things: sex and freedom, two aspects of life parents are afraid of, for some reason. We were never a band who was out to please the parents, because the problem with most parents is they forget they were ever young."

See? Nothing satanic. Don't try to tell me sex is satanic; if it is there are a lot of people in big trouble.

In Christ's Love,

M.M., Ohio

> *"Our philosophy has always been
> to do anything to become famous."*
> — *Dee Snider of* **Twisted Sister**

Chapter 9

Shock Treatment

Shock is defined in the **Webster's New World Dictionary** as "to affect with surprise; outrage or horrify." That is exactly why this chapter is written.

In the middle of 1984, the group **Motley Crue** was coming to San Antonio, Texas. The local rock radio station KISS-FM was doing some promotion for the concert. They were having a contest titled, "What would you do to see Motley Crue?" Listeners were invited to mail entries to the station stating exactly what they would do to get to see the group. The winners would get free tickets to the concert and some would get to go backstage and meet the band.

Upon hearing about the contest, Bob Greene, a contributing editor for **Esquire Magazine**, contacted the station and asked if he could see the entries for a possible story. What follows are some of his findings.

59

Some were deleted because of their tremendous immoral content.

From a 15-year-old girl:
"I want to see *Motley Crue* so bad that I'd wear black nail polish and body glitter. . .when I see them I'd get on my hands and knees and give them my body and even tear off my clothes if I had to. If that didn't work, I'd do like Ozzy did and bite a dove's head off and say, 'OK, let's talk business'. "

From a 13-year-old girl:
"I'd do it with the *Crue* until black and blue is all you see."

From a 16-year-old girl:
"First I would tie up (*Motley Crue*) spread-eagle and naked with leather straps. Then I'd shave all the hair off your chest and if I should nick you I'll suck up the blood as it slowly trickles over your body. Then I'll cover you with motion lotion to get things really heated up. Then I'll do things to your body you never thought were humanly possible. . .and when you're begging for more I'll slowly walk away and tell you I'm not that kind of girl."

From a 14-year-old boy:
"I would give them my mother who is very beautiful. She has red hair and brown eyes. She loves heavy metal, especially *Motley Crue*. My mother definitely has 'looks that kill'. "

The 13-year-old girl, who said she would "do it" with the band until she was black and blue had this to say to him, "I just love the group. I wrote what I wrote because 'they look like the type who would like that. They look like women lovers."

Then we have the 16-year-old girl who said she would tie up the members of the band naked and shave their chests, who told Mr. Greene, "I didn't let my boyfriend read it (the letter) before I sent it in. It would make him wonder what he didn't know about me. Why did I write those things? I don't know where the ideas came from."

When he spoke to this girl's mother, she told him, "Yes, I read the letter. Actually I took it down to the station for her. I guess I was shocked in a way, but I'm sure she didn't mean anything by it. She's a very good Christian girl. Did I think about not turning it in to the radio station? Well, it really wouldn't have been fair for me not to turn it in. I promised my daughter that I would do it. It wouldn't have been fair for me to put it in the garbage."

Lastly, we have the 14-year-old boy who said he would give them his mother. He said, "I wrote the letter because I really wanted to get to go backstage and meet *Motley Crue*. My mom likes the band too, and I thought if I offered her to them that I might have a good chance of winning. What if the band told me they really wanted my mother? I'd say, 'Take her,' and I'd say, 'Here'! I really love my mom: I know she'd go with them."

The boy's mother, who was 34, had this to say, "Yes, I am a fan of the band; I sure am. I approved of his letter. We keep listening to the radio to hear their music. They're kinda wild; just a little wild. Billy and I have a good mother and son relationship. He's crazy about me and I'm crazy about him. When Billy said that he offered me to the band I said, 'Oh Billy'! But I really do like them and I would like to help Billy win the contest."

I am sure that after reading these responses, "outraged and horrified" best describe the way you feel. The point that disturbs me most is that one of these letters comes from, what one mother referred to as, a "good Christian girl." Have our standards fallen so far that anyone who's ever worn a cross is considered to be a Christian? Many young people have even considered the perverted rock star *Prince* to be a Christian simply because he said, "thank God" when receiving an award! Why is it that the rock stars and cults are the only ones asking for a radical commitment from young people?

The time has come for redefining the word **Christian**.

In early Christianity, the commitment to Jesus Christ was so firmly established in the hearts of the believers that many of them were boiled in oil, burned at the stake, fed to the lions and even crucified. True Christianity takes man off the throne of his life and places Jesus Christ as supreme ruler and King of his heart. It changes man from being self-centered to being Christ-centered, looking for every opportunity to glorify God and live radically unselfishly in a selfish world.

These are the people that shine as lights in a dark world. They are salt in a world that has lost its taste, and reflectors of God in a God-hating and Christ-rejecting world.

A Christian is a person who is wholly committed to Jesus Christ and his rulership in their lives. They have been dethroned as the most important person in their lives and he now is seated on the most prized possession of their existence, their heart. He lives to please God and bring joy to his heart with every choice he makes. Without Christ he has no more purpose for existence. Why? Because "Christ is his life!"

How is it that we accept anyone who goes to church regularly, is moralistic, or speaks the Christian lingo, as being a Disciple of Jesus Christ? Is it because we want to call them Christians so we can excuse ourselves from total commitment and feel justified in our own carnality? After all, if that "so-called Christian" can be selfish, sensual and materialistic, then it's not too bad if I am the same way, right? Wrong! That person is not your example. Christ calls you to avoid any appearance of evil, whether it be to appear lustful, rebellious or pridefully trendy. Even more, he calls you to be spiritual and not self-centered.

Modern Christianity has conformed to the world, better known as carnal Christianity. This is not the Christianity of the Bible, which calls us to conform to the image of Christ, bearing about in our bodies the dying of our Lord Jesus Christ (dying to self), that the life of Jesus Christ may be shown through what we say and do.

Too often we see Christians that act like the world, look like the world, smell like the world and desire the things of the world. Isn't it time that we at least have the sense of a farmer? If it looks like a pig, smells like a pig, snorts like a pig and acts like a pig, then it's probably a pig.

How much longer can we convince worldly, selfish, sensual people they are Christians? The problem, as Leonard Ravenhill states, is not "eternal security but false security." How much longer can we continue to promise eternal life to people living only for selfish non-eternal values? How God must weep at our halfheartedness and love for everything but him.

'Oh, but I do love him,' you say. May I remind you that love is not a feeling but choosing the highest good for someone else, even at your own expense. That's what God did. God so loved the world that he gave his son. I'm sure he didn't emotionally feel like watching his son be mocked, rejected and crucified by the world, but he chose for our good even if it hurt him. That's real love...choosing for someone's good even at your own expense.

So you see, a Christian is not just someone who believes in Jesus. He is someone who is willing to lay down his life to follow him. Christ has not called you to give up your favorite rock or country group. He has called you to give up your life. Until we begin making him lord of all that we are, and become totally committed to radical Christianity, the church will remain lukewarm and cults and rock stars will continue to receive the radical commitment that really belongs to the Lord Jesus Christ.

The Solution

The solution to all of the above is a word almost forgotten in modern-day preaching: "repentance." It means you change your heart and mind about the choices you have been making and allow God to change your desires. True repentance is always followed by a change of desires. Instead of your choices following your feelings, your feelings follow your choices. If you're waiting for your feelings to change first, it may never happen. You change your choices and God will change your feelings.

Confess to God what you have done to him with

your selfish choices. Remember to be specific. You have made specific choices that have hurt God, so repent specifically for them.

Secondly, ask Christ to fill you with himself. You have been filled with yourself for so long, and now it's time to be filled with him (Christ).

Thirdly, tell someone about your commitment to follow Christ with your whole heart. It you have been lukewarm and are now committing yourself to be "Radical" for God, tell them.

Fourthly, get involved in a good local church. If you don't know of one in your area, write us and we will recommend one to you.

Fifthly, fall in love with God's Word, the Bible. If you have truly made a commitment to Christ, then he has placed a hunger in your heart for his Word.

Lastly, write me and tell me what Christ has done in your life so I can rejoice with you!

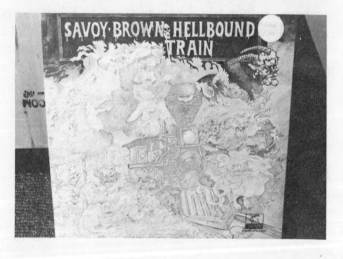

Top: **This group is called** *Satan.* **The album cover
shows the strong occultic influence in their music.**
Bottom: Savoy/Brown's **album** *Hellbound Train* **is
another example of the influence of the occult in rock
music.**

Top: The theme of *Ozzy Osbourne's* album *Bark at the Moon* is occultic. *Bottom:* A fan of singer *David Bowie* said, "... David Bowie is God."

Top: **Note the dress of** *Motley Crue* **for their** *Shout at the Devil* **album.** *Bottom:* **One of** *Motley Crue's* **songs is entitled "God Bless the Children of the Beast."**

"When you go on the road there's nothing to do but drugs and have sex."
— Steve Tyler of Aerosmith

Chapter 10

Behind The Scenes

Accept

Accept is Germany's new European group whose songs contain graphic discussions of gay sex and advocate revenge on its oppressors. Their latest album is titled *Balls to the Wall.* The album cover shows a man's leg and attempts to focus in on his crotch. Here are segments from some of their songs:

"Love Child":"...wrecking one's brain and I'm going insane / don't know why / I can feel your sex winding up the girl in the red dress..."

"Losers and Winners":"...why don't you take it easy and screw the girl who's next to you."

"Head Over Heels":"...gotta know who's out in the dark / I've stopped my breath / can feel the hands / could hear the sound of people making love..."

Adam and the Ants

Adam and the Ants, who rose to fame as an androgynous figure, likes to keep a sexual appeal to both men and women. In the May, 1984 issue of *Rock Fever*, Scott Trent interviewed Adam and asked him about some of the new and upcoming rock groups. "There's not enough sex and threat to them all...". He went on to say of the rock industry, "Gimmicks are only part of the best way to sell rock and roll. Sex and style are crucial too. That's what kids want. So I'm determined to be sexy and stylish. Sex is really an exciting part of rock and roll. When I dance onstage, I dance to turn people on (sexually). When I'm dancing, I turn myself on as well. Dancing is a sexual thing to do, you know" (*Rock Fever*, May 1984, pg. 13).

Inside the cover of his latest album *Strip*, Adam is featured nearly nude in a photo. One of the songs is titled "S.E.X." which states the following:

"And when the summer gets to me and sets
the sex on fire / my body is an ocean of twisted
white debris/ ...and sex is sex,
forget the rest."

Berlin

Berlin, with its hit song about "Sex (I'm a ...), might soon be the theme song of every porn/peep show/talk-to-a-live-model place in the country. Terri Nunn, the female sex symbol of the group, is the product of a father who studied Eastern religions and a mother who was an astrologer. By her own admission she stated, "I was always the corrupting influence in every friendship." They also have a song off the latest album *Love Life* titled "When We Make Love" (*Creem*, September 1984, pg. 46 & 64).

Top: Accept's album cover for *Balls to the Wall* has this very suggestive picture. *Bottom:* The album *Strip* by *Adam and the Ants* includes such songs as "Puss n Boots," "Strip," "Playboy" and "Navel to Neck."

David Bowie

David Bowie has been one of the prominent leaders in rock music over the past decade. He paved the way for bisexualities acceptance in rock music. Bowie openly admits his bisexuality, as well as his occasional dealing in black magic (witchcraft) (*Time Magazine*, July 18th, 1983). His former wife is a proud member of the gay (homosexual/lesbian) community.

Bowie has openly practiced backward masking. In recording his song "All the Young Dudes," he backward masked an entirely different song into it. When played backwards, "All the Young Dudes" becomes the song "Move On"!

His feelings about God are summed up in his song "Modern Love:"

> "Never gonna fall for modern love;
> walks beside me, modern love;
> walks on by, modern love;
> Get me to church on time,
> church on time terrifies me.
> Church on time makes me party;
> church on time puts my trust in God and man.
> God and man no religion.
> God and man don't believe in modern love."

Rolling Stone Magazine asked Bowie about his song "Alien," saying that is was out of the context of his album because it related to religion and history. He replied, "Yes, 'Alien' really doesn't fit in there, does it? That was the most personalized bit of writing on the album for me. . .That one was me in there dwelling on the idea of the awful s _ _ _ that we've had to put up with because of the church. That's how it started out. For some reason I was very angry."

The reporter responded by saying, "That's an odd thing to hear from someone wearing a crucifix."

"I know," answered Bowie, "the crucifix is strictly symbolic of a terrible, nagging superstition that if I didn't have it on, I'd have bad luck. It isn't even religious to me."

He went on to say, "The crushing thing about the church is that it has always had so much power. It was always more of a power tool than anything else, which was not very apparent to the majority of us" (*Rolling Stone*, October 25, 1984, pg. 18).

Boy George and the Culture Club

Many viewers watching the 1984 Grammy Awards were shocked to see a guy dressed like a girl by the name of Boy George. After winning the New Group of the Year Award, Boy George told the audience, "Thank you, America. You know a _ _ _ _ good drag queen when you see one."

Boy George, born in 1961 as George O'Dowd, was the third son of a large Irish-Catholic family in south London. By the time he was 14 years old, he was escaping from home to the festive halloween spirit of London's gay bars. After a number of simple jobs, George was offered a spot in a group called *Bow Wow Wow* by the manager of *The Sex Pistols*. As a result of his disagreements with members of the group, he left to form a new band called *The Sex Gang Children*, who later changed their name to *The Culture Club* (*Time Magazine*, January 23, 1984; *The Brownsville Herald*, April 15, 1984).

In France he was held up at customs because they didn't believe he was a boy (***Rolling Stone***, March 15, 1984).

He also refused to submit to any sex test. When asked about sex, George's response was, "Having sex with boys or girls is like eating a bag of crisps (potato chips) to me. It's irrevelant in that I don't have to think about it" (***Rock Fever,*** March 1984, pg. 27).

His song, "Church of the Poison Mind," was meant to impugn the bigotry of organized religion. Recalling his early childhood, he relates the story of being in church when his little brother pulled down his pants. His mother was so embarrassed that they never went back to church again.

"I was very pleased about that," he says.

Boy George has even been so sacrilegious as to dress up in a nun's habit. His actions make it clear that he means what he says when he professes, "I don't believe in God: we all go into the earth and come back as maggots and that sort of thing."

About his confused sexual identity, Boy George said, "I admit that from the age of 16 I have fancied (been attracted to) both men and women. But sex has never been an obsession with me. However I think I'll end up with a woman, because I would love to have children" (***London Sunday Magazine***).

In another more recent interview with the famed ***Rolling Stone Magazine***, when asked about sex, Boy George replied by saying, "I've said I'm bisexual and that's enough of an explanation. It's 1984. People shouldn't be bothered about this stuff. My sex life is very important and very private to me. I enjoy having sex. Most of my male lovers have been kind of casual things. Men are very different to have relationships with" (***Rolling Stone***, June 7, 1984, pg. 14).

Top: When *Boy George* received a 1984 Grammy Award the audience was amazed to see him dressed like a girl. His album *Colour by Numbers* includes "Karma Chameleon," "Victims" and "Church of the Poison Mind." *Bottom:* Here also dressed in "drag" this *Culture Club* album includes a song entitled "I'm Afraid of Me."

The Cars

The Cars, with their stylish leader Rick Ocasek at the steering wheel, have been Boston's biggest contribution in years to new music trends. The group has just released their latest album *Heart Beat City*. Popular reviews of the album reveal that it's an album about drugs.

When asked if the real content is indeed drugs, Ocasek responded by saying, "It could be, and it probably is in the sense that I'm writing about relationships around me, and in those relationships people probably were...I mean...I don't do drugs anymore, but I see a lot of people using them to live. And the songs do contain references to the fact that I know people who are so wrapped up in drugs that they can't see anything else" (*Rolling Stone*, July 19, 1984, pg. 108).

Other songs by *The Cars* are sex-related like "You're All I've Got Tonight," and "Lust For Kicks." Perhaps the group's sexual views are expressed in the song "You're All I've Got Tonight," where it says, "you can pump me / I don't care / you can bump me / I don't care / You can love me / just about anywhere."

John Cougar Mellencamp

John Cougar presently has warrants out for his arrest in three states for profanity (*Rock*, April, 1984, pg. 5).

Cougar, who grew up in a small town in Indiana, could probably be best described as one of rock's greatest rebels.

In one interview, he said, "I swear because I know it's not socially acceptable."

He went on to say, "I hate things that are this-is-the-way-you-are-supposed-to-behave. That's why I hate schools, governments, and churches" (**People**, October, 1982).

He described his years of growing up in Seymour, Indiana, like this, "I hung around with a real tough group of guys. We were the ones who were always fighting and getting kicked out of basketball games. I was the one who was out drinking, getting laid (having sex), and getting in trouble" (**Hit Parader**, May 1984, pg. 26).

His rebellion is clearly heard in his "Authority Song": I fight authority / authority always wins / I been doing it since I was a young kid / and I've come out grinning. So I call my preacher / and I say give me strength for round five / he said, you don't need no strength, you need to grow up son. / I said, growing up leads to growing old and then to dying / and dying to me don't sound like all that much fun.' "

One of his songs, which expresses his view of heaven and hell, is the song "Golden Gates" which says, "I don't need to see a woman crying for the Savior / holding onto some money-man's hand / Who can I call to make reservations / forever thrown in the dark."

Much of Cougar's music is also sexual. His first hit song was "I Need a Lover." Then, off his John Cougar **Uh-Huh** album came "Serious Business": "This is serious business / sex, violence, and rock and roll (repeat). Take my life, take my soul, put me on the cross for all to see / put my name around my neck / let those people throw stones at me / this is serious business / sex, violence, and rock and roll."

Another sexual-related song is "Hurt So Good": "With a girl like you / Lord knows there are things

Top: **Some of the lyrics of songs by** *The Cars* **have sexual and drug overtones.** *Bottom:* **John Cougar says he hates "schools, governments and churches." Much of his music is sexual as this album cover so expresses.**

we can do baby / just you and me / come on baby, make it hurt so good (repeat) / you make it hurt so good."

In one of his songs, "Crumblin' Down" he says, "No, no, I never was no sinner."

Really?

Def Leppard

Def Leppard is one of the hottest new masters of heavy metal music. With an average age of just 22 for its members, **Def Leppard** is considered to be a very young band. The first effort by the group was an album released in 1978, financed by the leader of the band, Joe Elliott and his parents. The title of the album was *Getcha Rocks Off*, which refers to having a sexual orgasm. Pete Willis, former member of the group, was allegedly kicked out of the band because of his tremendous drinking problem (*Hit Parader*, 1984, pg. 22).

When describing the message in their music, Elliott responded by saying, "Heavy metal, after all, unless you're trying to make some political message is party music."

He added, "It's escapism: you come home from work, and it's nice to hear somebody sing about girls and beer. It's a lot more fun to find different things than politics to sing about, even if it's different women. You know, ten songs, ten women, that's not bad" (*Hit Parader*, July, 1984, pg. 37).

Dio

Ronnie James Dio, formerly with the group *Black Sabbath*, is known for using the patented satanic salute.

The salute is given by extending the index finger and smallest finger so that they look like horns. This is supposed to ward off evil spirits and spells. This symbol can also be seen being used by Anton LaVey, the "black pope" and head of the Church of Satan, on the back of the satanic bible.

Dio has always entertained a satanic image. On his album *Holy Diver,* the cover shows a demonic creature with horns. This creature has his hand in a satanic salute. His other hand holds a chain which is wrapped around a minister wearing a clerical collar and the minister is drowning in the water because he is bound with the chain. This supposedly shows evil winning over good.

Duran Duran

Duran Duran is another of the very youthful groups that has invaded America with a pop sound and sexual appeal. Even though this group is very young, they realize that sexual appeal is what can put you on top.

Simon Le Bon of the group made that clear when he said, "You gradually find out what makes you look good; especially what appeals to women. It's not so much what you make yourself look like; it's an attitude you have towards women in your mind" (*Teen Beat,* Fall, 1983, pg. 6).

Eurythmics

The **Eurythmics** basically consist of two people: David Steward and Annie Lennox. Her bisexual appeal rode in on the same wave that brought us Boy George.

Describing how they met, David said, "The first day

This is the cover of *Def Leppard's* album *Pyromania.* Joe Elliott, the leader of the band said their music is escapism. "... you come home from work, and it's nice to hear someone sing about girls and beer ... you know, ten songs, ten women, that's not bad."

Ronnie James Dio, formerly with the group *Black Sabbath*, is known for using the patented satanic salute. Dio has always entertained a satanic image. On his album *Holy Diver* the cover shows a demonic creature with horns.

I met Annie, we moved in together. . .we didn't say anything about it, we just naturally assumed that's the way is was" (*Record*, October, 1983, pg. 17).

Annie's bisexual, or transvestite, approach is so convincing that while recording the video *Sweet Dreams* for MTV, she had to send over her birth certificate to prove she was a woman! (*National Examiner*, April 17, 1984).

When asked about her looks, she responded by saying, "Some people have thought that I was a transvestite because I'm tall and I used to wear brassy stuff. I like the transvestite look" (*Rock Fever*, July, 1984, pg. 31).

During an interview with *New Sound Magazine*, Dave Steward was asked what he thought about all the adoration the *Eurythmics* were receiving.

"Actually, I spend a lot of time thinking about sex," he said. In the same article he confessed that he and Annie have spent up to three hours having their fortunes told by a tarot card reader. When asked what else they should talk about in the interview, Dave responded, "Let's talk more about sex and things like it!" (*New Sound*, January, 1984, pg. 12).

Frankie Goes To Hollywood

Frankie Goes to Hollywood is a British group that is openly homosexual. They have succeeded in making homosexuality fashionable in Britain, and would like to do the same in the United States.

Holly Johnson of the group told *Rolling Stone Magazine*, "We're not waving any banners. If I'm interviewed now, it's as a musician. If I want to be gay after tea time, it's entirely my affair."

The Gap Band

Ronnie, Charlie and Robert Wilson are the three brothers who are known as *The Gap Band*, and considered to be black music superstars. Up to this point, they have sold close to five million albums. In truth, they are the backslidden children of Reverend Oscar Wilson, a Pentecostal minister. Ronnie, Charles, and Robert were raised in Tulsa, Oklahoma, in the Church of God in Christ denomination. Raised in a Christian home, they have now ended up battling drugs and sexual immorality.

Ronnie almost lost his mind because of cocaine addiction. Charlie was quoted as saying, "I try to leave kids wherever I go," referring to the women he's left pregnant along the way. One thing is sure: success will never fill the gap this band has! They need to get right with God and begin singing where they first started out...in church! (quotes from *Rolling Stone*, March 1, 1984, pg. 44).

Gatlin Brothers

Larry, Steve, and Rudy Gatlin have risen to the peak of country music popularity and success. These three brothers had a simple start in their hometown of Odessa, Texas; not as country singers, but as gospel artists singing to share the love of Jesus Christ.

Larry eventually began to sing and tour with one of the most famed gospel groups in America, *The Imperials*. Larry's sister, Ladonna, is married to one of the members of *Dallas Holm and Praise*, with whom she also sang for a few years. To state it mildly, Larry has fallen far from the faith that first compelled him to sing.

Top: Duran Duran is a youthful group with a pop sound and sexual appeal. They realize it was this sexual emphasis that put them on top. *Bottom: Annie Lennox of the Eurythmics* has a bisexual appeal and also has the transvestite approach to her music.

Larry recently turned himself in at a drug abuse center for rehabilitation. Some of *The Gatlin Brothers'* songs are self-explanatory by their titles: "Night Time Magic," "I Wish You Were Someone I Love," and one of their latest songs "If there's no Mogen David in heaven, then who the hell wants to go."

Marvin Gaye

Marvin Gaye is another sad story of someone who left singing in the church to sing for the world. Marvin was the son of a minister who became so enraged during a heated argument that the life he helped bring into the world, he took away. Marvin was dead after his father shot him twice with a pistol. Marvin's problems were many, from drugs to divorce.

"He became beastlike while under the influence of cocaine," his father stated in an interview (*Lafayette Advertiser*, April 8, 1984).

Many of Marvin's songs were sexually related like "Let's Get It On," "You Sure Love To Ball," "Distant Lover," "Come Get To This," and his last number one hit, "Sexual Healing."

Grim Reaper

Grim Reaper, new to America, has been together for some 10 years in England. Their image is satanic and occultic. Their two albums are titled, *See You in Hell* and *Fear No Evil*.

Following is a segment from *See You in Hell:*
"See you in hell / can I make you an offer you can't refuse? / I keep my eyes on you 'cuz I tell you that you lose / now you can come with me to a place you know so well / I will take you to the very gates of hell."

Nina Hagen

Nina is a German singer who, from what she says, seems to be a medium for some occultic power.

"I saw my first witch sitting under the table when I was three years old," says Nina.

At age 17 she had an "out of the body experience" during an acid trip, at which time (she claims) that a representative of God's named Micky "borrowed" the body of the non-tripping friend taking care of her. Nina and God had a talk. Since that time, Hagen's albums and life have been filled with her..."version of the moon upstairs. My music is spiritual food" (*Creem*, August, 1984, pg. 15).

Merle Haggard

Merle Haggard was born in California, though his father was from Oklahoma. He grew up in a train boxcar. At age nine, he watched his father die of a brain hemorrhage. From that time on, Merle was a delinquent.

He has been charged with theft, assault, attempted burglary and eventually ended up in San Quentin Penitentiary for three years. He has since earned notoriety by gambling, staying wired (high on drugs) on speed, and being married a number of times. He also confesses, "I smoke grass (marijuana) and I party a lot" (*US*, November 21, 1983, pgs. 52-53).

Hall & Oates

Two years ago, John Oates and Daryl Hall were voted the top pop group of the year, although their musical career began in the early '70s. Their first

Frankie Goes to Hollywood has succeeded in making homosexuality fashionable in Great Britain and would like to do the same in the United States. They are openly homosexual in their lifestyles and performances.

The Gap Band - which has three black music superstars - are the sons of a Pentecostal minister. Although they were raised in a Christian home, they now are battling drugs and sexual immorality.

album on RCA records (for whom they still record) was released in 1975. It featured a controversial cover showing Daryl and John made up in an androgynous (bisexual) style. Inside the album cover, John posed nude. This is nothing new for *Hall & Oates.*

Daryl Hall has said, "The first time I ever heard myself on radio I was making out with my girlfriend in a basement. And I was heavy into the middle of something deep (referring to the act of sex). Suddenly, the record came on, and I jumped up and screamed. There was no sex once that record started."

In the same interview, Hall also admits to being involved sexually with men while at a younger age. In bolder moments, he states, "The idea of sex with a man doesn't turn me off" (*Rolling Stone*, January 17, 1985, pg. 20).

Billy Idol

Billy Idol, whose real name is William Broad, was born the son of a traveling salesman. Billy spent four years of his childhood in Rockville Centre, Long Island. His family then returned to their original home in England.

In Billy's teenage years, he became a punk rocker and eventually started a punk rock group by the name of *Generation X*. It was just prior to this that William changed his name to "Billy Idol," claiming, "I can be an idol just by calling myself one."

Generation X later broke up and Idol went solo. Punk rock eventually hit America and Billy Idol is riding the crest of its wave. His music is filled with sex, drugs and rebellion. He doesn't hesitate to brag of his sexual adventures: "One night it's great _ _ _ _ _ some bird (girl), one night it's great getting a _ _ _ _ ."

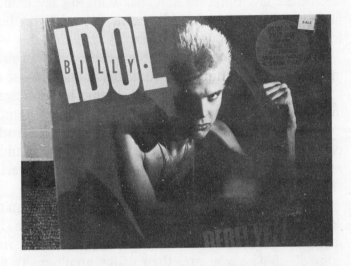

Billy Idol (top and bottom) sings music that is filled with drugs, sex and rebellion. He even brags about his sexual adventures.

One evening Billy was in a restaurant in Cleveland, Ohio, and said to a passing girl, "Would you be interested in some unhealthy sex?"

Then Billy got up from the table and escorted the girl into the men's bathroom where she performed oral sex on him while he sang, "Rebel Yell," one of his hit songs that refers to having sex.

Idol has also been known to stand up in public and pull his pants down like he did in one Manhattan restaurant, exposing himself to everyone there (*Penthouse*, December 1984).

When asked about drugs, Idol said, "Drugs don't really alter your perception or anything that much. I mean they do, but I think if you feel pretty much in control of who you are, then drugs aren't really a problem" (*Song Hits*, May 1984, pg. 15).

During an autograph session in a Hollywood record store, one of Billy's female fans wanted his signature, so he signed one of her breasts and then sealed it with a kiss (*People Magazine*, April 9, 1984, pg. 103).

Billy was asked the question, "Do you see yourself being a father?"

His response was, "That sort of thing happened by mistake in the past. So I don't know. It's already bad enough as it is, without planning it" (*Rock Fever,* May, 1984, pg. 42).

Billy pleaded guilty of assaulting a 20-year-old girl in a Henrietta, New York, motel after a concert. She reported that Idol bounced her off the wall in his motel room (*Creem*, August 1984, pg. 14).

Iron Maiden

Iron Maiden was formed in 1977 and two years later released its first album.

Although this group was a headlining band in England, it wasn't until their third album, *The Number* *of the Beast*, that they became a main attraction in America.

The group readily admits that they are into witchcraft; but the truth of the matter is that they are dabbling in the occult.

The bass player, Steve Harris, claims that occultic things fascinate the band, but they don't want to get too deeply involved because there's too much they don't know about it (*Creem*, September, 1982, pg. 44).

Their fascination with the occult has seemed to blossom with their latest album, *Powerslave*. The concept for the album came from the mind of Bruce Dickenson, the leader of *Iron Maiden.*

He explains, "The Egyptian idea came about because of my interest in religion and magic and all that weird sort of stuff...my reading habits are inclined towards that sort of thing. A lot of stuff has its background in Egypt and its civilization. The idea of *Powerslave* is to try and get enough magic on the album so that it'd maybe rub off on the whole event" (*Hit Parader*, April, 1985, pg. 4).

The stage for their new "World Slavery Tour" will have an Egyptian motif, complete with sarcophagus (stone coffin), replicas of Isis (the occultic Egyptian goddess of fertility), and her mate Osiris (occultic son of the earth, sky and husband of his sister, Isis; also god of the dead).

It is quite interesting that this group has attempted to bring Egyptian roots into their new album.

"To people of antiquity, as well as of the modern world, Egypt appeared as the very mother of magic" (*Encyclopedia of Occultism and Parapsychology*, pg. 285).

As much as this group would like to avoid it, they seem to still be deeply influenced by the occult.

Dickenson said in a 1984 interview, "When I wrote 'Flight of the Icarus', I tried to bring in some modern elements of those themes, and in other songs we've referred to things like the tarot (occultic tarot cards), and the ideas of the people like Aleister Crowley" (*Circus*, August 31, 1984, pg. 82).

Mick Jagger

Mick Jagger, leader of the legendary rock group *The Rolling Stones*, has recently recorded his first solo album titled *She's the Boss*. An hour-long video, made to promote the album, features Mick in "drag" (dressed as a woman), and actress Rae Dawn Chong in next-to-nothing, according to *People Magazine*.

Nudity is hardly new to Chong, who appeared in the caveman epic *Quest for Fire*.

"I was naked for 16 weeks in the movie," she said. "But even a veteran disrober can feel some discomfort."

Before her taping segment with Jagger, says Chong, "I asked the director to point out where each of Mick's kisses should go on my body" (*People Magazine*, February 25, 1985, pg. 27).

"It's not that I throw my clothes off at the drop of a hat, but I really love bodies. I love having sex. I grew up in a really free environment. We didn't have boyfriends, we had each other's boyfriends" (*Rolling Stone*, April 11, 1985).

Rae is the daughter of Tommy Chong, from the well-known comedy team *Cheech and Chong*.

Immorality is nothing new to veteran rocker Jagger, whose first wife, Bianca, claimed, "Mick was dissolute when it came to women. All my friends slept with

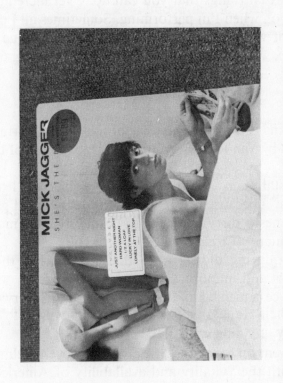

Mick Jagger sometimes dresses in "drag" (as a woman). He recently fathered a child with his live-in girlfriend. "Sometimes all I can think of when I get off stage is finding someone to have sex with," he is quoted as saying.

him" (*Creem*, September, 1982, pg. 13).

Mick's present live-in girlfriend has recently made him a papa once again. Yet there still seems to be no plans for Jagger to marry her.

Jagger has been quoted as saying, "Performing onstage in front of all those large crowds is one of the most sexual things that you can do. I get incredibly turned on when I'm performing. Sometimes all I can think of when I get off stage is finding someone to have sex with" (*Hit Parader*, December, 1983, pg. 61).

Krokus

Krokus is a Swiss heavy metal rock band, formed in 1974 by Van Rohr, who was later kicked out of the group.

As stated in his own words, "I had to leave Krokus...because my general attitude included giving honest, dirty interviews as the band's main spokesman" (*Circus*, July, 1984, pg. 60).

His quitting didn't mean that *Krokus* left their dirtiness and immoral implications behind.

Storace, a member of the group, said in the interview about their Hungarian tour, "Girls were willing to do virtually anything for a Hershey bar."

He went on to say that the group was overwhelmed also with the "vitality and availability of American girls."

"Girls in America have the right idea when it comes to dealing with musicians. They just want to have a good time and not to worry about anything as trivial as a lasting relationship," he said.

Storace ended the interview by saying, "My favorite new song (off their latest album) is 'Long Stick Goes Boom' whose lyrics say, 'My stick is tight / my blood is hot / let's do it right now on the spot." I don't know if we're as sexually blatant as some people say, but if we are, at least we're singing about something we enjoy" (*Hit Parader*, Fall 1982, pg. 26).

Marc Storace of *Krokus* claims he's convinced that his vocals are possessed by <u>some strange force</u> when the rest of the band starts playing.

"You can't describe it," says Marc, "except to say it's like a mysterious energy that comes from the metaphysical plane and into my body. It's almost like being a medium, conducting the energy and using bits of it" (*Circus*, January 31, 1984, pg. 70).

Cyndi Lauper

Cyndi Lauper was born on June 20, 1953, into an Italian-American family. At a young age she was sent to a convent school in New York City's borough of Queens, where she was raised. She rebelled furiously against the Holy Trinity Church, family and state.

"You know what I learned?" Cyndi stated. "Those are the three biggest oppressors of women that will ever come along" (*Newsweek*, March 4, 1985, pg. 50).

Cyndi seems to portray herself as a woman who would like to lead a revolution for the ERA. She resents the role of a woman with simple traditional values. Perhaps this is why the liberal *MS.* magazine named Lauper as one of its women of the year last January!

Lauper also confesses to having been involved with alcohol and drugs (*People*, September 17, 1984, pg. 87).

Also noteworthy is Lauper's song "She Bop" which is her tribute to masturbation.

Krokus is a heavy metal rock band formed in Switzerland. One of the band's members said of their Hungarian tour: "Girls were willing to do virtually anything for a Hershey bar." He went on to say that the group was overwhelmed with the "vitality and availability of American girls." He added: "Girls in America have the right idea when it comes to dealing with musicians."

Madonna

Madonna Louise Veronica Ciccone is the third child of eight and the oldest daugher of an Italian-Catholic family from Pontiac, Michigan.

During her junior year of high school, Madonna "dropped out of cheerleading, pierced her ears, got into nuts and berries, and stopped shaving her armpits and legs," says her high school chum, Mary Conly Belote.

Others who knew her remember her as a very worldly sort of girl who frequented gay bars.

Madonna has left a tidal wave of affairs behind her, the longest being an adulterous live-in relationship with New York DJ, "Jelly Bean" Benitez.

In 1979, Madonna acted in her first movie, an underground film titled *A Certain Sacrifice.* In the movie, Madonna plays the part of a quasi dominatrix, who has three sex slaves, then a boyfriend.

Before the movie's over she's raped by yet another admirer. Although the movie's not hard-core pornography, there's a lot more seen than Madonna's familiar belly button.

During the MTV Rock Video Awards, Madonna descended from the top of a gigantic wedding cake dressed in all white, and began to sing her hit song "Like a Virgin." Tossing back a bridal veil to reveal a strapless gown, she then laid down on the stage and began to writhe her body.

This sensual escapade by Madonna promised more than an invitation to dance. All this is not just an accident. Madonna seems most comfortable when exposing as much of her bust and body as MTV will allow. Madonna confessed in an MTV interview, "Sex is part of my image."

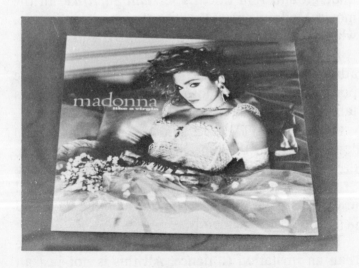

Madonna (top and bottom). "As long as I'm riding high on the charts, I don't care if they call me trashy, a tart or a slut. I'm proud of my image," she says.

She added: "As long as I'm riding high on the charts, I don't care if they call me trashy, a tart or a slut. I'm proud of my trashy image" (*Globe*, June 6, 1985, pg. 37).

Her song, "Like a Virgin," is about a girl who has been used sexually. She falls in love and the boy she's in love with makes her feel "shiny and new" again, like a virgin.

Here are some of the words:
"I'd been had, I was sad and blue;
But you made me feel, yeah, you made me feel
shiny and new, like a virgin,
touched for the first time, like a virgin.
When your heart beats next to mine,
gonna give you all my love, boy."

Here are a few segments from other Madonna songs:
"Dress You Up":"... gonna dress you up in my love, all over your body."

"Shoo-Bee-Doo":"...'cause the boy with the cold hard cash is always Mister Right."

"Burning Up":"...unlike the others I'd do anything: I'm not the same, I have no shame; I'm on fire. You know you got me burning up, baby, burning for your love."

"Physical Attraction":"...You say that you need my love; all you're wanting is my body; I don't mind, baby, all I've got is time. And I'm waiting to make you mine, but you say you wanna stay the night, but you'll leave me tomorrow. I don't care, all your moves are right."

Missing Persons

The group *Missing Persons* was formed in 1980 and is fronted by lead singer Dale Bozzio. She was a Playboy Bunny for two years in Boston before becoming interested in the punkish sound that the group still maintains (**Lafayette Daily Advertiser,** September 15, 1984).

The group claims their appeal is not only to the ears, but also to the eyes.

Motley Crue

Motley Crue was formed in 1981. Most of the members were brawling street rebels from the Los Angeles area.

"We were all troublemakers who were thrown out of school before we graduated," one of the group says.

 To describe what *Motley Crue's* values are is simple: sex, drugs and Satan.

On the subject of sex, Nikki Sixx of the group says, "We like women of all sizes, but sometimes the fat, ugly ones are the best . . . they're willing to do anything. What American youth is about is sex, drugs, pizza and more sex."

Vince Neil of the group confessed, "I'm obsessed with sex, fast cars and faster women. Paradise to me is a room full of long-legged blondes and a waterbed" (*Rock Fever,* May, 1984, pg. 43).

Nikki also said of 10 girls who were attempting to attack him after a concert, "Take numbers and wait your turn" (*Hit Parader,* April 1985, pg. 26).

In yet another article, they admitted that they didn't know if they were more sore after an autograph session or from all the sex they were involved in the evening before.

When notified by one interviewer that their album *Shout at the Devil* was doing good, Nikki Sixx stated, "I'm not surprised that our records are selling well. All we have to do is have every woman we've

_ _ _ _ (had sex with) buy our record and it's guaranteed to go platinum" (*Hit Parader*, Fall 1984, pg. 31).

Just listen to the titles of some of their songs: "Helter Skelter," "God Bless the Children of the Beast," "Red Hot," and "Ten Seconds to Love," a song written by Nikki Sixx.

He said, "It's one of my favorites on the album. If you listen closely, you can hear a lot of squishing sounds during the song. That's because we were_ _ _ _ _ (having sex) with some chicks while we were making the record. Now when they play the song at home they can tell their friends, 'Hear that noise? That's me _ _ _ _ _ _(having sex) with Nikki Sixx' " (*Hit Parader*, December 1983, pg. 36).

They have declared many times, "We are the grossest band in rock and roll history."

The symbol they use for the group is a pentagram, which is a symbol of Satan's power.

When speaking of their stage show, Nikki said, "We have skulls, pentagrams, and all kinds of satanic symbols on stage. . .I've always flirted with the devil" (*Circus*, January 31, 1984, pg. 70).

Judas Priest

Judas Priest is best known for their heavy metal gut-wrenching sound. *Judas Priest* may sound like an awkward name, but not when you consider that Rob Halford's original band was named **Lord Lucifer**.

Their latest album is titled *Defenders of the Faith*. When questioned about the title of this album, Rob, the lead singer, responded by saying, "We're defending the faith of heavy metal music" (*Hit Parader*, May, 1984, pg. 16).

One of their albums was advertised by saying *"Judas Priest* has sin for sale."

Another one of their publicity shots, featured in *Hit Parader* of October 1982, showed all five members of the group mimicking sex with a girl that only had on a bra and underpants.

K.K. Downing of the group stated in an interview, "The only way to relieve those frustrations are with your girl in the back seat. If you can't get a girl, a guitar makes a wonderful substitute" (*Hit Parader*, Fall 1982, pg. 31).

Another time he states, "The guitar is very sensual. When I play it, it's like making love."

 Glenn Tipton of the group also said, "I just go crazy when I go onstage. . .it's like someone else takes over my body" (*Hit Parader*, Fall 1984, pg. 6).

One *Rolling Stone Magazine* reviewer said some of the content of their latest album was laced with sado-masochism.

Michael Jackson

Michael Jackson, formerly of **The Jackson 5**, became a living legend with the release of his *Thriller* album. *The Guinness Book of World Records* named it the largest selling album of all time. By the end of 1984, the album had sold 25 million copies worldwide.

Looking into Michael's personal life, it is a known fact that he is a very devout member of the non-Christian cult called the Jehovah's Witnesses. This cult rejects salvation through Christ and him alone. They even maintain their own personal translation of the Bible. It is also well known that Michael is a financial supporter of the Jehovah's Witnesses and contributes money he's earned from his profession to the cult.

So if you've purchased any Michael Jackson music posters, or other paraphernalia, you've helped him support this anti-Christian cult! Next time they come knocking at your door, you could open it and say, "I already gave money to your cause." I'm sure that would be a real thriller!

The girl who played opposite Michael in the video *Thriller* is none other than Ola Ray featured in a revealing spread in the pornographic magazine *Playboy* (*Class*, August, 1984, pg. 22).

Some of Michael's music is also sexually oriented. The song "Body," off their victory tour album, says, "Girl I want your body / girl I need your body / girl I want your body / won't you come home with me?"

John Lennon

John Lennon had one of the most powerful influences on rock music. He, along with his group *The Beatles*, helped to shape the values and philosophy of an entire generation of young people.

In 1974, John Green, an occultist, was hired by Yoko Ono (Lennon's wife) to be her tarot card reader. As time went on he became Lennon's advisor, confidant and friend. Until October of 1980, he worked closely with them. They did everything according to "the cards" (occultic tarot cards). He advised them on all of their business transactions and investments, even to the point of how to handle the problems Lennon was having with Apple, *the Beatles* record company (*Song Magazine*, February 1984, pg. 16).

Ted Nugent

Ted Nugent, better known as the 'Motor City

Madman,", has been pounding out rock music publicly for 15 years.

His latest album is titled **Penetrator.**

Much of Nugent's content in his songs is sexual. Songs like "Wang Dang Sweet Poontang" and "Cat Scratch Fever," are typical of Ted Nugent.

While speaking in a recent interview about his latest album **Penetrator,** he said, " We did this album out in L.A.'s record plant because it's fairly inexpensive, and once you've finished working for the day the _ _ _ _ _ (sex) hunting's great. That's how I know my music is going. If the _ _ _ _ _ (sex) hunting's good, I know I've done a good day's work. Those ladies can just sense the sweat and inspiration that I've put into a day's work, and they want to come and relax me. I like L.A. because the _ _ _ _ (sex) out there is young and clean. You don't have to worry about catching any unwanted social diseases" (**Hit Parader**, April, 1984, pg. 25).

Ozzy Osbourne

Ozzy, as he is known to his devoted followers, started on the rock scene in the late sixties as the leader and front man for the satanic heavy metal group **Black Sabbath**. While in **Black Sabbath**, Ozzy seemed to continually be tinkering with witchcraft and the occult. Since leaving **Black Sabbath**, Ozzy has continued in his quest for mixing rock and the occult.

 On his album **Blizzard of Oz,** he even sang a song about one of the greatest male satanists (or warlocks) who ever lived: Aleister Crowley!

Yes, it's hard to believe that biting the head off of bats, and urinating in public at the Alamo are not enough to entertain Ozzy.

Michael Jackson's release *Thriller* (above) is the biggest-selling record album of all time having sold 25-million copies by the end of 1984. Some of his music is sexually oriented.

Speaking of his latest stage show, Ozzy says, "It's a mixture of magic and mysticism" (*Hit Parader*, April, 1984, pg. 22).

I recently received a call from a young lady whose brother committed <u>suicide</u> while listening to Ozzy's song "Suicide Solution."

The Pretenders

The Pretenders, headed up and led by Chrissie Hynde, released their first album in 1980. The album became a hit and everything seemed wonderful.

Later, Chrissie met Ray Davies of the *Kinks*, and their immoral relationship produced a child. On June 14, 1982, the group was forced to fire the bass player, Pete Farndon, who had formed the group along with Chrissie. Pete had been a junkie (heroin addict) since 1978. Two days later, guitarist James Honeyman-Scott died at age 25 when his own drug and alcohol abuses got the best of him, particularly cocaine (*Creem*, August, 1984, pg. 30).

All of these events have caused Chrissie to begin looking for answers, but apparently in the wrong places. Her reading material during a recent tour was Bhagavad Gita, a Hindu-type bible used by the cult, The Hare Krishnas.

In a *Rolling Stone* interview, she stated that there was a time when she was so fueled by drugs and alcohol that she would do or say just about anything.

"I had some bad experiences," she told *Rolling Stone*. "But the way I look at it, for every act of sodomy I was forced to perform, I'm getting paid 10,000 pounds (British money) for now" (*Rolling Stone*, April 26, 1984, pg. 19).

Prince

Prince Rogers Nelson is the son of John Nelson, a half-black musician.

He was named Prince after his father's stage name.

After his father left the family, Prince began to direct all his energy toward music. He eventually moved in with his father, but was later kicked out because of his loud guitar playing.

As a result, he moved in with the Cymones, his best friend's family. Here, studying his music, he was exposed to a local promoter, Owen Husney, who eventually persuaded Warner Brothers executives to listen to a demo tape by Prince. The rest of the story is history.

Most of Prince's music is sexual. He seems to be obsessed with a warped sense of morality.

In an interview talking about his view of sex, he said, "When I was nine, I wanted to write pornographic novels. My mother used to keep a lot of pornographic material in her bedroom and I used to sneak in there and read it. This had a great deal to do with my sexuality today. It made me warped to a degree, but it made me aware of my sexuality at an early age" (*New Sounds*, January 1984, pg. 20).

Andre Cymone, his best friend that he was raised with, stated of Prince, "Prince's crazy thing was passing girls around. We shared maybe twenty, maybe more." Cymone also detailed some adventures, like the time Prince tied a girl to the ceiling after blindfolding her (*Rock Fever*, July, 1984, pg.6).

When Prince was asked about the meaning of some of his songs he had this to say:

"Sister": a song about incest he shared with

his sister.
Prince: "Sister is pretty self-explanatory. It's not pro-incest. It's just an experience. It should not be taken any other way but that. It's just an incident in my life. It's real" (meaning he did have sex with his sister).

"Uptown": a song about homosexuality.
Prince: "Uptown was a song about a state of mind everyone has, but is afraid to show; an openness to things people don't understand. The song takes the example of homosexuality and deals with the way we, the band, feel about life; that we're open and do whatever we want."

"Head": A song about oral sex.
Prince: "In the song Head, the girl is about to get married so she wants to stay a virgin. She'll only let the guy in the song give her head (oral sex). It's so good, she decides to give up marriage" (*New Sounds*, January, 1984, pg. 20).

Other of Prince's songs speak of used Trojans, (condoms).

His latest album, *Purple Rain*, features a song, "Darling Nikki." Part of the song says: "I knew a girl named Nikki / I guess you could say she was a sex fiend / I met her in a hotel lobby / masturbating with a magazine. . ."

In his song "Delirious," the final stanza says: "Girl u gotta take me for a little ride / up and down, in and out and around your lake / I'm delirious."

As if all of this wouldn't be enough, Prince now uses backwards masking to mock the return of Christ.

Most of *Prince's* music is sexual and he seems to be possessed with a warped sense of morality. He said his song *"Sister"* is about incest he shared with his own sister.

The Police

The Police, headed by singer-bassist Sting, have established themselves as one of the top new sounds of the '80s. Sting confessed to being involved with drugs from the time he was 12 years old, until he was 31.

In 1982, Sting separated from his wife, actress Frances Tomelty. He is presently living in adultery with girlfriend Trudie Styler who recently gave birth to his child.

When asked in a recent interview if he was considering marriage, he said, "I'm not a ball-and-chain man..."

He went on to say, "I don't see the point" (referring to marriage); "one can procreate without the dreaded ritual" (*US* Magazine, March 25, 1985, pg. 30).

Sting seems to enjoy the idea of being a sex symbol.

"Being a sex symbol is quite fun," Sting admitted, "but it has nothing to do with selling records. It means I can enjoy myself when I'm stuck in Minneapolis."

In the same interview he confessed, "I am terribly good in bed and I want people to know that" (*Hit Parader*, July 1982, pg. 28).

In a 1984 interview, Sting spoke of Christianity as "the Christian myth" (*Seventeen Magazine*, January 1984, pg. 110).

The Police's latest hit song is titled "Wrapped Around Your Finger."

In the second verse of this song it says, "Mephistopheles is not your name. But I know what you're up to just the same. I will listen hard to your tuition, and you will see it come to its fruition."

The term "Mephistopheles" is the name of a demon with whom, according to legend, a man named Faust signed a pact. He gave his soul to the devil in exchange for youth and honors. He practiced magic (witchcraft), invoked spirits, and claimed to have ridden through hell. At the time of this pact, the devil caused him to suffer a horrible death (***Dictionary of Satanism***, pg. 219, 131).

Quiet Riot

Quiet Riot was formed by Kevin DuBrow in 1975. They broke up, and were re-formed in the early 1980s.

When asked about the image of the group, one of them said, "We want to have the image of party insanity."

Perhaps that's why they posed in a recent issue of *Hit Parader* in just their underwear!

In a ***Rolling Stone*** interview, Kevin DuBrow said, "When we get off stage, we run up and down the hallways naked and slap girls around."

Rudy Sarzo, another member of the group, stated his reasons for becoming a rocker in ***Quiet Riot***.

"I was a chunky, sexually depraved kid, and the reason I got into music was because of all the girls." He went on to say that the best place he ever played in his career was a topless club.

Quiet Riot also has backwards masking on their *Metal Health* album.

A segment played backwards says, "Serve the beast for money."

One of their songs, "Sign of the Times," says "We've got street-sense radar / we're supposed to be bad news / you better lock up your daughters / you never know what we'll do."

Ratt

Ratt, a Los Angeles-based quintet, has been together for three years. The name of the band was originally *Mickey Rat,* which is the name of an X-rated comic book.

One interviewer spoke of the odor found on the bus that Ratt is touring in by saying it "smelled of stale cigarettes, bras, and assorted unmentionables from female admirers, dangled everywhere like hunting trophies" (*Hit Parader,* April 1985, pg. 52).

Speaking of the girls who followed them, one said, "We don't bring naked girls onstage. We leave them at home...or backstage...or hotel rooms" (*Hit Parader,* July 1974, pg. 28).

Scorpions

The Scorpions are the first German heavy metal rock group ever to receive worldwide recognition. Most of their music is based on sexuality.

Albums like *Animal Magnetism, Love Drive* and *Virgin Killers,* express the values of this group.

On the original cover of "Virgin Killers" was a photo of a naked 10-year-old girl sitting among pieces of jagged broken glass. Her legs were spread open and arrows pointed to her private parts with "Virgin Killers" blazed across the album.

Their latest album, *Love at First Sting,* shows one of the members of the group supposedly having sex with a topless woman straddled across him.

When speaking of the new album, Klaus Meine of the group said his favorite song was "Rock You Like

Speaking of the admiring girls who follow them, one Ratt member said, "We don't bring naked girls onstage. We leave them at home . . . or backstage . . . or hotel rooms."

A Hurricane."

He explains it's "the story of going out on the road and looking for a little love, especially at first sting (referring to sex). It talks of what life on tour is like for us. It's strange waking up in some strange city with a new cat (girl) lying next to you every day, but it's something we've gotten used to (*Hit Parader*, May, 1984, pg. 21).

Following are the words to Meine's favorite song, "Rock You Like A Hurricane": "It's early morning / the sun comes out / last night was shaking and pretty loud / My cat is purring and scratches my skin / so what is wrong with another skin? / The bitch is hungry / she needs to tell, so give her inches and feed her well / More days to come, new places to go / I've got to leave / it's time for a show / Here I am / rock you like a hurricane." (Sounds like an orgy anthem!)

One thing that slowed down the recording of *Love at First Sting*, complained Klaus, was drummer Herman Rarebell.

"Herman was in horrible shape," added Klaus, "I don't know if it was too much drugs or too much ------ (sex), but he had a total breakdown" (*Hit Parader*, May, 1984, pg. 21).

Another member of the group, Rudolf Schenker, said of one of their concert crowds, "I think we have good taste and a good audience. They aren't too much into herpes. . ."

On rock and roll philosophy, Klaus told *Rolling Stone Magazine*, "I prefer making love with a girl instead of a dog."

Klaus told *Hit Parader*, "Rock and roll is a very sensual form and we're a very sensual band" (*Hit Parader,* January 1984, pg. 6).

Sheila E.

Sheila E. is a female Prince protege whose break in the music industry came because of her association with Prince.

She, like Prince, enjoys performing on stage, and she wears only sexy lingerie.

"I get inhibited when I wear too much clothes onstage," said Sheila. "It cuts down on my mobility. I want the audience to know there's a woman onstage. My femininity enhances my music. I can be sensual through my songs" (*USA Today*, October 1, 1984).

In one of Sheila's concerts, her dancing and sexual antics became so energetic that she popped out of her blouse, according to *Rolling Stone Magazine.*

Sheila's hit song "The Glamorous Life," which is filled with sexual gyrations on the MTV video, says, "Boys with small talk, small minds, really don't impress me in bed. . ."

Rick Springfield

Rick Springfield is an Australian-born actor and singer. With three platinum albums, and five top-ten singles, Rick has proven he is serious about his music. Rick also stars in the popular soap opera "General Hospital."

In a recent movie, *Hard to Hold*, he spends the first five minutes of the movie running around half-naked with a towel over the front of his body and nothing on the back. Before the movie is over, he is involved in fornication (premarital sex) everywhere, from in front of the fireplace to the park. Scenes like this make it easy to see why Rick Springfield would be "hard to hold"!

Sheila E. performs on stage in sexy lingerie. "I can be sensual through my songs," she says. Her hit "The Glamorous Life" - in the MTV video version - is filled with sexual gyrations.

In his recent movie *Hard to Hold*, Rick Springfield spends the first five minutes of the movie running half-naked. Before the movie is over he is fornicating everywhere - from in front of the fireplace to the park.

When asked in a recent interview if he relied on any personal experience for the movie, he said, "Yes...I drew on different things that happened to me in my life, as any other actor does."

When asked about drugs, in the same interview, he responded, "I've tried different drugs, but I was never reliant on them. If I felt like I was doing too much of anything, I would just stop" (*Family Weekly*, April 15, 1984, pg. 17).

When referring to his acting and singing in a 1982 interview, Rick said, "To me, they're two different approaches to exorcising the demons inside me" (*Hit Parader*, June, 1982, pg. 14).

One of his songs, "Jessie's Girl," relates his own fantasizing about his friend Jessie's girlfriend.

One verse says, " 'Cause she's watchin' him with those eyes and she's lovin' him with that body / I know it/ and he's holdin' her in his arms late, late at night. . ." It continues . . . "I want Jessie's girl."

Segments from another one of his songs, "I Get Excited," says, "Oh baby stay / we've got all night, all night / baby please, I can please you / from on my knees tonight / This angel gonna spread her wings tonight . . ."

Bruce Springsteen

Bruce Springsteen was born in 1949 in Freehold, New Jersey, the first of three children.

Bruce's own account of his life says that he was dead until rock and roll changed his life. His concerts have become somewhat of a church service.

Bruce begins his concert, "Welcome to the first church of the rock, brothers and sisters."

Then the Reverend Bruce gets into his preaching rap.

Bruce Springsteen's rock concerts try to mock church services. He shouts "Do you believe if you die during the course of this concert, due to excitement, that you're going to heaven?" He says he was dead until rock and roll "saved" him.

Waving his arms and assuming his best Sunday morning mode (he likes to watch TV evangelist Jimmy Swaggart).

He intones: "Do you believe that if you die during the course of this show, due to excitement, that you're going to heaven?"

He then begins to tell stories about how he almost became a baseball player until rock 'n' roll saved him (*People Magazine*, September 3, 1984, pg. 70).

All this can be nothing more than Bruce mocking the gospel and true Christianity.

Tina Turner

Tina Turner, formerly of *Ike and Tina Turner*, has divorced her husband and gone solo.

Live on stage, Tina is just one step away from a striptease show, displaying endless sexual movements and gyrations. Her low-cut tops, and endless slits in her dresses have become one of Tina's trademarks.

Her song, "What's Love Got to Do With It?" revived her dying career and launched her out of the ranks of black soul music into pop and rock stardom.

Her album *Private Dancer* has sold over seven million copies.

In a recent interview on ABC's program *20/20*, she was asked why she felt she was appealing to the younger generation.

"The world is rebellious," she replied, "That's why I joined the young crowd."

She went on to confess that she was a practicing Buddhist and that you could change your life by chanting. She also spends quite a bit of time reading about the occult and astrology.

On stage, *Tina Turner* is just one step away from a striptease show, displaying endless sexual movements. She spends a lot of time offstage studying the occult and astrology.

Van Halen

Van Halen is easily the most popular "heavy metal" rock band in America today. The ingenious guitar wizardry of Eddie Van Halen and the sexual antics of lead singer David Lee Roth are the trademarks of the band.

Touring with *Van Halen* could best be described by their song "Running With The Devil"! David Lee Roth boldly proclaims "rock and roll is more than music, it's a lifestyle;" and who should know better than David Lee Roth, the first man to publicly attempt to insure his genitals with Lloyds' of London for at least $10,000 (*Record*, April 1984, pg. 30).

This is nothing new for Roth who already has "paternity insurance" for any girls he may get pregnant on the road (*Creem*, September 1982, pg. 29).

Roth boasts, "Whatever somebody else can't do in his 9-5 job, I can do in rock and roll."

He continued, "When I'm on stage with volume rippling my body like a glass of water and thousands of people are generating heat in my direction, there's no time for thought. My basement faculties take over completely."

When Roth speaks of this sexual escapades, he delights in the fact that his first sexual experience came when he was 14 years old on a Pacific isle.

When referring to how many girls he's been involved with, Roth stated, "I don't keep records, but when we go on the road, especially to other countries, I feel like I'm sort of a goodwill ambassador of the United States. It's my duty to meet as many of the natives as I can, especially females, and impart part of myself."

Roth continued, "A lot of people think a *Van Halen* tour is just one long orgy with a few stops on stage in-between. Well let me tell you, they're right!" (*Rock*,

Top: *Van Halen* undoubtedly is the most popular "heavy metal" rock band in America today. The ingenious guitar wizardry of Eddie Van Halen and the sexual antics of lead singer David Lee Roth (Bottom) are the trademarks of the band.

April 1984, pg. 12).

When describing what a *Van Halen* concert is like Roth replied, "It's like therapy; we're gonna see through these emotions and I'm gonna act them out for you."

He told the interviewer, "I'm gonna abandon my spirit to them, which is actually what I attempt to do. You work yourself up into that state and you fall in supplication of the demon gods. . ." (ibid, pg.30).

Roth openly declares that "rape and pillage play important parts in rock and roll". . .and. . ."yeah (I'm) toastmaster for the immoral majority."

In one concert, Roth's sexual antics so aroused a female fan she ran onstage and pulled down Roth's pants.

Roth also claims to be involved in the cultic Zen (a sect of Buddhism) (*Hit Parader*, July 1984, pg. 33).

 Here are some of the titles from *Van Halen's* songs: "Feel Your Love Tonight," "Spanish Fly," "House of Pain," "Hot For Teacher," "Running With The Devil," and "Everybody Wants Some."

Vanity 6

Vanity 6, which is now **Appollonia 6**, sported their first album in 1982.

This group, who can even boast of *Purple Rain Fame,* is known for performing in skimpy lingerie.

Here are the words to some of their songs. . . "Nasty Girl": ". . .it's been a long time since I had a man that did it real good. If you ain't scared, take it out." "Wet Dream": ". . .he's my number one star, my wet dream." "Drive Me Wild": ". . .I'll do anything, I'm the best . . . come on baby, drive me wild."

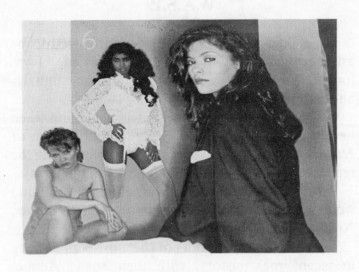

Vanity 6 - now ***Appollonia 6*** - can boast of performing in skimpy lingerie. Some of their song titles are
"Nasty Girl," "Wet Dream" and "Drive Me Wild."

W.A.S.P.

When Blackie Lawless, the leader of the group, was asked how he formed the group, he responded, " I was looking for the closest thing to penitentiary inmates and I think I found them."

Chris, of the group, claims Lawless met him when he saw his picture in the "Beaver Hunt' section of *Hustler Magazine* (Beaver Hunt is a section where the readers send in their own nude shots or pictures).

W.A.S.P. is also known for bringing naked, bound women on stage during live concerts (*Hit Parader*, April 1985, pg. 74).

They are also the authors of the most-banned song in recent rock history, with their song "Animal _ _ _ _ _ (have sex) Like a Beast."

In another interview, when Blackie was asked what it is about heavy metal that appeals to people, he replied, "For me it's always been the energy. I like Willie Nelson, but his music doesn't make me want to get up and beat the snot out of somebody; it just doesn't get the frustrations out. When you take adolescence, which is painful at best, and put in a heavy dose of hostility, you've got a lethal combination, buddy. And you put a bunch of 'em out there and you better believe they're volatile."

Willie Nelson

Willie Nelson has become one of country music's largest legends of all time. His appeal is not only country-oriented, but many rockers idolize Nelson.

Willie Nelson, like many others in country music, was **first** exposed to religious music. Willie was raised by his grandparents and it was his grandfather who

W.A.S.P. is known for bringing naked, bound women on stage during live concerts. They are also the authors of the most banned song in recent rock history -- about sex with animals.

gave him his first guitar at the age of 10. His grandmother wrote gospel songs, and at a very early age he began writing too.

Willie has fallen a long way from gospel themes. He now confesses to believe in reincarnation and believes he has progressed from a previous lifetime. His beliefs come out clearly in his song "Karma."

Karma is the totality of one's acts in each state of existence of each one of their lives as believed by the Buddhists.

Here's a segment of "A Little Old-Fashioned Karma Coming Down": "There's a little old-fashioned Karma coming down. Just a little old-fashioned justice going round. A little bit of sowing, a little bit of reaping, a little bit of laughing and a little bit of weeping. Just a little old-fashioned Karma."

Other books I would like to recommend on rock music are:

Why Knock Rock
by Steve and Dan Peters
Bethany House Publishers

The Legacy of John Lennon
By David A. Noebel
Nelson Publications

Rock N' Roll and the Occult
By Joel Landis Ministries
P.O. Box 6304
Linglestown, Pa. 17112

The God of Rock
By Michael Haynes
Priority Publishers
P.O. Box 1254
Lindale, Texas 75771

To contact Jacob about coming to speak at your church, or other function, write:

Aranza Outreach
P.O. Box 1330
Lindale, TX 75771

Tapes available by Jacob Aranza are listed below and can be obtained by sending $5.00 for each tape and specifying the tape desired:

Rock 1
Rock 2
Rock 3
(This is Jacob's entire rock seminar)

Backward Masking 1
Backward Masking 2
(Satanic messages of all the latest rock groups exposed)

A Reasonable Reason to Wait
(a 90-minute message on sex before marriage by Jacob; you will laugh and you will cry while listening to this message!)

MORE FAITH—BUILDING BOOKS
BY HUNTINGTON HOUSE

AMERICA BETRAYED! *by Marlin Maddoux.* This hard-hitting book exposes the forces in our country which seek to destroy the family, the schools and our values. This book details exactly how the news media manipulates your mind. Marlin Maddoux is the host of the popular, national radio talk show "Point of View."

A REASONABLE REASON TO WAIT, *by Jacob Aranza,* is a frank, definitive discussion on premarital sex — from the biblical viewpoint. God speaks specifically about premarital sex, according to the author. The Bible also provides a healing message for those who have already been sexually involved before marriage. This book is must reading for every young person - and also for parents - who really want to know the biblical truth on this important subject.

BACKWARD MASKING UNMASKED, *by Jacob Aranza.* Rock and roll music affects tens of millions of young people and adults in America and around the world. This music is laced with lyrics exalting drugs, the occult, immorality, homosexuality, violence and rebellion. But there is a more sinister danger in this music, according to the author. It's called "backward masking." Numerous rock groups employ this mind-influencing technique in their recordings. Teenagers by the millions - who spend hours each day listening to rock music - aren't even aware the messages are there. The author clearly exposes these dangers.

BACKWARD MASKING UNMASKED, (cassette tape) *by Jacob Aranza.* Hear actual satanic messages and judge for yourself.

BEAST *by Dan Betzer.* This is the story of the rise to power of the future world dictator - the antichrist. This novel plots a dark web of intrigue which begins with the suicide-death of Adolf Hitler who believed he had been chosen to be the world dictator. Yet, in his last days, he spoke of "the man who will come after me." Several decades later that man, Jacque Catroux, head of the European economic system, appears on the world scene. He had been born the day Hitler died, conceived by the seed of Lucifer himself. In articulate prose, the author describes the "disappearance" of the Christians from the earth; the horror and hopelessness which followed that event; and the bitter agony of life on earth after all mortal and spiritual restraints are removed.

DEVIL TAKE THE YOUNGEST *By Winkie Pratney.* This book reveals the war on children that is being waged in America and the world today. Pratney, world-renowned author, teacher and conference speaker, says there is a spirit of Moloch loose in the land. The author relates distinct parallels between the ancient worship of Moloch - where little children were sacrificed screaming into his burning fires - to the tragic killing and kidnapping of children today. This timely book says the war on children has its roots in the occult.

GLOBALISM: AMERICA'S DEMISE, by William Bowen, Jr. The Globalists - some of the most powerful people on earth - have plans to totally eliminate God, the family, and the United States as we know it today. Globalism is the vehicle the humanists are using to implement their secular humanistic philosophy to bring about their one-world government. The four goals of Globalism are • A ONE-WORLD GOVERNMENT • A NEW WORLD RELIGION • A NEW ECONOMIC SYSTEM • A NEW RACE OF PEOPLE FOR THE NEW WORLD ORDER. This book clearly alerts Christians to what the Globalists have planned for them.

GOD'S TIMETABLE FOR THE 1980'S, *by Dr. David Webber.* This book presents the end-time scenario as revealed in God's Word. It deals with a wide spectrum of subjects including the dangers of the New Age Movement, end-time weather changes, outer space, robots and biocomputers in prophecy. According to the author, the mysterious number 666 is occurring more and more frequently in world communications, banking and business. This number will one day polarize the computer code marks and identification numbering systems of the Antichrist, he says.

MURDERED HEIRESS...LIVING WITNESS, *by Dr. Petti Wagner.* The victim of a sinister kidnapping and murder plot, the Lord miraculously gave her life back to her. Dr. Wagner - heiress to a large fortune - was kidnapped, tortured, beaten, electrocuted and died. A doctor signed her death certificate, yet she lives today!

NATALIE, THE MIRACLE CHILD *by Barry and Cathy Beaver.* This is the heartwarming, inspirational story of little Natalie Beaver - God's miracle child - who was born with virtually no chance to live - until God intervened! When she was born her internal organs were outside her body. The doctors said she would never survive. Yet, God performed a miracle and Natalie is healed today. Now, as a pre-teen, she is a gifted singer and sings the praises of a miracle-working God.

REST FROM THE QUEST, *by Elissa Lindsey McClain.* This is the candid account of a former new Ager who spent the first 29 years of her life in the New Age Movement, the occult and Eastern mysticism. This is an incredible inside look at what really goes on in the New Age Movement.

TAKE HIM TO THE STREETS, *by Jonathan Gainsbrugh.* Well-known author David Wilkerson says this book is ". . . immensely helpful . . ." and ". . . should be read. . ." by all Christians who yearn to win lost people to Christ, particularly through street ministry. Effective ministry techniques are detailed in this how-to-book on street preaching. Carefully read and applied, this book will help you reach other people as you **Take Him to the Streets.**

THE AGONY OF DECEPTION, *by Ron Rigsbee.* This is the story of a young man who became a woman through surgery and now, through the grace of God, is a man again. Share this heartwarming story of a young man as he struggles through the deception of an altered lifestyle only to find hope and deliverance in the grace of God.

THE DIVINE CONNECTION, *by Dr. Donald Whitaker.* This is a Christian guide to life extension. It specifies biblical principles for how to feel better and live longer. Dr. Whitaker says you really can feel better and live longer and shows you how to experience Divine health, a happier life, relief from stress, a better appearance, a healthier outlook on life, a zest for living and a sound emotional life.

THE HIDDEN DANGERS OF THE RAINBOW, *by Constance Cumbey.* A national #1 bestseller, this is a vivid expose' of the new Age Movement which is dedicated to wiping out Christianity and establishing a one-world order. This movement - a vast network of tens of thousands of occultic and other organizations - meets the test of prophecy concerning the Antichrist.

THE HIDDEN DANGERS OF THE RAINBOW TAPE, *by Constance Cumbey.* Mrs. Cumbey, a trial lawyer from Detroit, Michigan, gives inside information on the New Age Movement in this teaching tape.

THE MIRACLE OF TOUCHING, *by Dr. John Hornbrook.* Most everyone enjoys the special attention that a loving touch brings. Throughout the chapters of this encouraging book the author explains what touching others through love - under the careful guidance of the Lord Jesus Christ - can accomplish. Dr. Hornbrook urges Christians to reach out and touch someone - family members, friends, prisoners and do it to the glory of God, physically, emotionally and spiritually.

THE TWISTED CROSS, *by Joseph Carr.* One of the most important works of our decade, **The Twisted Cross** clearly documents the occult and demonic influence on Adolf Hitler and the Third Reich which led to the Holocaust killing of more than six million Jews. The author even gives the specifics of the bizzare way in which Hitler actually became demon-possessed.

WHO WILL RISE UP? *by Jed Smock.* This is the incredible - and sometimes hilarious - story of Jed Smock, who with his wife Cindy, has preached the uncompromising gospel on the malls and lawns of hundreds of university campuses throughout this land. They have been mocked, rocked, stoned, mobbed, beaten, jailed, cursed and ridiculed by the students. Yet this former university professor and his wife have seen the miracle-working power of God transform thousands of lives on university campuses.

Yes, send me the following books and/or tapes:

___ copy (copies) of **America Betrayed!** @ $5.95 = _____

___ copy (copies) of **A Reasonable Reason To Wait** @ $4.95 = _____

___ copy (copies) of **Backward Masking Unmasked** @ $4.95 = _____

___ copy (copies) of **Backward Masking Unmasked**
        Cassette Tape @ $5.95 = _____

___ copy (copies) of **Beast** @ $5.95 = _____

___ copy (copies) of **Devil Take The Youngest** @ $6.95 = _____

___ copy (copies) of **Globalism: America's Demise** @ $6.95 = _____

___ copy (copies) of **God's Timetable for the 1980's** @ $5.95 = _____

___ copy (copies) of **More Rock, Country & Backward**
        Masking Unmasked @ $5.95 = _____

___ copy (copies) of **Murdered Heiress. . Living Witness** @ $5.95 = _____

___ copy (copies) of **Natalie** @ $4.95 = _____

___ copy (copies) of **Rest From the Quest** @ $5.95 = _____

___ copy (copies) of **Take Him to the Streets** @ $6.95 = _____

___ copy (copies) of **The Agony of Deception** @ $6.95 = _____

___ copy (copies) of **The Divine Connection** @ $4.95 = _____

___ copy (copies) of **The Hidden Dangers of**
        the Rainbow @ $5.95 = _____

___ copy (copies) of **The Hidden Dangers of the Rainbow**
        Seminar Tapes @ $13.50 = _____

___ copy (copies) of **The Miracle of Touching** @ $5.95 = _____

___ copy (copies) of **The Twisted Cross** @ $7.95 = _____

___ copy (copies) of **Who Will Rise Up?** @ $5.95 = _____

Enclosed is $_____ including postage.

Send check/money order or for faster service VISA/Mastercard orders call toll-free 1-800-572-8213. Add: Freight and Handling, $1.00 for the first book ordered, 50¢ for each additional book.

AT BOOKSTORES EVERYWHERE - or order direct from: Huntington House, P.O. Box 53788, Lafayette LA 70505.

Name: _____

Address: _____

City: _____ State: _____ Zip: _____